THE
MAN
WHO
FOUND
NINEVEH

BOOKS BY ROBERT SILVERBERG

Nonfiction

The Man Who Found Nineveh
Great Adventures in Archaeology
The Great Doctors
Home of the Red Man: Indian North America Before
    Columbus
Empires in the Dust
Fifteen Battles that Changed the World
Sunken History: The Story of Underwater Archaeology
Lost Cities and Vanished Civilizations
Treasures Beneath the Sea

Science Fiction

Time of the Great Freeze
Collision Course
Lost Race of Mars
Revolt on Alpha C

THE MAN WHO FOUND NINEVEH

THE STORY OF AUSTEN HENRY LAYARD

BY ROBERT SILVERBERG

HOLT, RINEHART AND WINSTON

NEW YORK / CHICAGO / SAN FRANCISCO

And he will stretch out his hand against the north, and destroy Assyria; and will make Nineveh a desolation, and dry like a wilderness. And flocks shall lie down in the midst of her, all the beasts of the nations: both the cormorant and the bittern shall lodge in the upper lintels of it; their voice shall sing in the windows; desolation shall be in the thresholds: for he shall uncover the cedar work. This is the rejoicing city that dwelt carelessly, that said in her heart, I am, and there is none beside me: how is she become a desolation, a place for beasts to lie down in! every one that passeth by her shall hiss, and wag his hand.

—Zephaniah 2:13-15

About the year 1829, an English boy named Henry Layard, not quite twelve years old, lay stretched on the floor of the fabulous Rucellai palace in Florence, reading as fast as his eyes could travel over the pages. Hour after hour, he lay sprawled under a gilded Florentine table in the huge palace his parents had rented, gobbling up the gaudy tales of djinns and caliphs found in *The Arabian Nights*.

Sinbad and Aladdin, Ali Baba and Scheherezade, all the magical old stories danced in the boy's head. His mind whirled with thoughts of the parched desert, of the fabled towers of Baghdad, of the desert sheikhs in their flowing robes, of flashing scimitars and sumptuous feasts.

Another of Henry's favorite sets of books was the long row of novels by Sir Walter Scott, whose exciting stories were the best-sellers of the day. Young Henry Layard read not only *Ivanhoe* and *Kenilworth*, but also those glamorous romances of the Near East, *The Betrothed* and *The Talisman*. Scott's words brought to vivid, glowing life the sun-baked world of the Orient, with its castles and brigands and wandering desert tribes. The tales of adventure in Arab lands kindled something in Henry's imagination, lit a blaze that never went out.

"To them," he wrote many years later, "I attribute that love of travel and adventure which took me to the East, and led me to the discovery of the ruins of Nineveh." The famous old stories of Aladdin and Ali Baba and the Crusaders would all one day come alive for Henry Layard—

who was lucky enough to visit the scenes of *The Arabian Nights* at a time when something of their authentic flavor still lingered in the East.

For in the East lay Henry Layard's destiny—in the fabled land of Mesopotamia. That boy of not quite twelve, his eyes ablaze with the bright wonders of his storybooks, grew to manhood with that romantic flame still glowing. Eastward he went, toward Baghdad and Constantinople, and toward the ugly, crumbling, unromantic mounds of earth that concealed the ruins of a bygone civilization.

When a traveler of the nineteenth century passed through the part of the world that today is called Iraq, one physical feature above all else came repeatedly to attention: high mounds of earth, heaped up here and there over the face of the land. In the north, these mounds centered around the city of Mosul, on the River Tigris. In the south, they clustered about Baghdad, on the Euphrates.

Among the many Europeans who came to visit this part of what was then the Turkish Empire, and who stared at the strange mounds in curiosity and awe, was that dashing, adventurous young Englishman named Henry Layard. Layard, hardly out of his twenties when he first spied the mounds in the desert, wandered everywhere, saw everything, missed no chance to ask questions of the natives.

"What are these mounds?" he wanted to know.

"They are the cities of the ancient ones," came the answer.

Cities? These shapeless heaps of rubble? The mounds were sprawling clumps of earth, covered with grass, cloaked in spring with a brilliant array of flowers. The tireless, inquisitive Englishman prowled over the mounds. Winter rains had formed ravines down their sides, laying bare their contents. And—yes—there were hints that these mounds had once been the sites of the dwellings of men.

For near the surface of them lay fragments of pottery, and bits of alabaster, and bricks inscribed in strange, wedge-shaped characters. Within might lie the walls of palaces, the tombs of the ancients, the ruins of a vast civilization.

Layard decided to have a look.

He began to dig in 1845, and what he found not only was history, but made new history. Layard came upon the ruined cities of Assyria, three thousand years old. When his reports of his findings reached Europe, they touched off excitement and wonder, and inspired other men to journey eastward in search of the secrets of lost yesterdays. Layard was one of the first, and one of the greatest, of all archaeologists. He is a towering pioneer of the science that has restored so much of man's forgotten past.

This is his story—the story of the birth of Assyriology.

c. 4000 B.C.—Sumerians enter Mesopotamia, conquer primitive occupants, and establish a great civilization.

c. 2400—Sargon I invades Sumer and establishes his own empire, which lasts about a century.

c. 1800—Rise of Babylonia under King Hammurabi.

c. 1300—Rise of Assyria as important rival to Babylonia.

1280-1261—Rule of Shalmaneser I of Assyria, builder of Calah (Nimroud).

1250—Tukulti-Ninurta I, King of Assyria, defeats Babylonia and imprisons the Babylonian king. Babylonia soon independent again.

c. 1100—Tiglath-Pileser I of Assyria conquers Babylonia and makes her a province of Assyria.

885-859—Reign of Assurnasirpal, Assyrian king who built the Northwest Palace found by Layard at Nimroud.

858-824—Reign of Shalmaneser III, Assyrian king shown on the black obelisk of Nimroud.

721-705—Reign of Sargon II, Assyrian king who built the city of Dur-Sharrukin (Khorsabad) first excavated by Botta.

704-681—Reign of Sennacherib, Assyrian king who built the palace uncovered by Layard at Kouyunjik. Destruction of Babylon during this reign.

680-669—Reign of Esarhaddon, Assyrian king who built

the Southwest Palace found by Layard at Nimroud. Restoration of Babylon in Esarhaddon's reign.

668-626—Reign of Assurbanipal, Assyrian king whose library at Nineveh was found by Hormuzd Rassam.

625—Babylon rebels against Assyria and becomes an independent city under Nabopolassar.

612—Army of Persians and Medes lays siege to Nineveh and conquers it. The city is burned. Assyrian Empire destroyed and its lands divided among Medes, Persians, and Babylonians.

604-562—Reign of Nebuchadnezzar, King of Babylonia. Babylon rebuilt into world's most splendid city.

538—Persian army under Cyrus conquers Babylon. End of independent Babylonian kingdom.

A.D. 1811—Claudius Rich makes first modern investigation of ruins of Babylon.

1820—Rich visits mounds at Mosul, said to be ruins of Assyrian city of Nineveh.

1840—Austen Henry Layard pays first visits to ruins at Mosul and Baghdad (Nineveh and Babylon) but does not excavate.

1843—Paul Emile Botta excavates successfully at Khorsabad (Dur-Sharrukin).

1845—Layard begins to excavate at Nimroud (Calah).

1846—Layard begins to excavate at Kouyunjik (Nineveh).

CONTENTS

    I. "I AM HENRY LAYARD" / 1

   II. THE LONG WAY TO CEYLON / 10

  III. DAMASCUS TO BAGHDAD / 25

  IV. THE REALM OF THE SHAH / 40

   V. TO BAGHDAD, BAREFOOT / 51

  VI. SECRET AGENT LAYARD / 61

 VII. NIMROUD / 71

VIII. WINGED BULLS AND BEARDED KINGS / 86

  IX. PROBLEMS AND PLEASURES / 97

   X. A BULL TO THE RIVER / 108

  XI. NINEVEH! / 118

 XII. CONTROVERSY AND CUNEIFORM / 125

XIII. THE PALACES OF NINEVEH / 137

XIV. THE ROYAL LIBRARY / 152

 XV. LAYARD GOES TO BABYLON / 161

XVI. FAREWELL TO MESOPOTAMIA / 169

XVII. LAYARD AFTER ASSYRIA / 175

XVIII. ASSYRIA AFTER LAYARD / 190

     BIBLIOGRAPHY / 201

     INDEX / 203

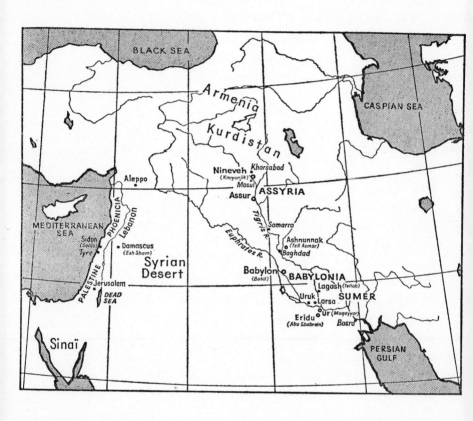

I

The Layards were of French Protestant stock, but had fled to England in the seventeenth century to avoid religious persecution. Daniel Peter Layard, born in 1720, was a noted physician, an antiquarian, and an author, who made a fortune in the practice of medicine and wasted almost all of it in a vain attempt to prove that he had a right to the title of Baron Camville, which he thought had belonged to his family in the fourteenth century.

Dr. Layard had three sons. Two of them became generals in the British army; the third entered the church. The churchman, known as Dean Layard of Bristol, lived well, according to his grandson's account: "He frequented good society, enjoyed a good dinner, and drank freely of port— which probably brought on the malady that caused his death. He seems to have cared little for his children. His sons were apparently a trouble and an embarrassment to him. He placed them, when very young, with decent country families—farmers, I believe, or persons in that station of life—to be brought up in a healthy fashion without much regard to learning."

Two of Dean Layard's neglected sons made their way, in 1796, to the far-off island of Ceylon, at the southern tip of the Indian Peninsula. Ceylon had just been ceded to England by the Dutch, and many young Englishmen headed there in search of fame and fortune, among them Henry Peter Layard and his younger brother Charles.

Charles remained, but Henry Peter found the climate

too much for his fragile health. He retired on a small pension and returned to England, where he married his childhood sweetheart, a small, beautiful, blue-eyed woman who was the daughter of the well-to-do banker Nathaniel Austen.

Not long after their marriage, the Battle of Waterloo wrote finis to the stormy career of Napoleon, and restored peace to troubled Europe. The Layards took advantage of the return of peace to travel abroad, and they were in Paris, on March 5, 1817, when the future discoverer of Nineveh was born to them in a hotel in the Rue Neuve des Petits Champs. They named him Henry Austen Layard.

The elder Layard suffered from asthma, contracted while in Ceylon. England's dank, foggy climate was bad for his health, and his doctor recommended residence in sunny Italy. In 1820 the Layards—now numbering five, since two more sons had arrived—departed from England to live in Pisa.

En route, they stopped off in Paris. Young Henry, then three, was taken to the zoo, and promptly horrified his nurse by picking up a lion cub and cuddling it! The cub's mother looked on in surprise, while Henry's brother Frederic howled in fear. In Geneva, he watched an eclipse of the sun; he remembered, years later, being shown the eclipsed sun through a piece of smoked glass.

The Layards lived in Pisa a short while, and then moved on to Florence, where they remained for several years. Henry began his schooling there, but, he tells us, "I learnt little at my school except the alphabet. I was, I believe, very idle, self-willed, and troublesome, and I know that I passed the greater part of my time in the corner, or lying on the floor with a backboard—a punishment I much disliked and resented."

His early friends thought of him as good-natured and amiable, but somewhat quick-tempered—characteristics that remained his all his life. He was happiest wandering in the hills near Florence, picking wild flowers or trying to catch songbirds.

Henry's father, who had acquired a taste for art, took him to see the museums and galleries that are Florence's great glory. From his earliest years, then, Layard's love of art was cultivated and developed.

Three more boys were born to the Layards in Florence, but only one survived. At the urging of the Austens, the whole family returned to England so that the four boys could be educated in British schools, but again the elder Layard found the climate oppressive. The Layards were off again, this time for France. Henry remained behind at school in England for a while.

When he was eight, his father sent for him. Young Layard made the trip from England to France alone—the first of his many journeys. He arrived safely and was enrolled in a French school, where he suffered from the jeers and taunts of his classmates. England and France had been bitter enemies for centuries, and the scars of the recent war had not yet healed. English boys were anything but popular in French schools in 1825.

As tough and resilient as he was good-natured, Henry survived the rough treatment of his classmates, and even seems to have thrived on it. He grew up self-reliant, unafraid, and able to handle himself in any kind of unpleasant situation.

A good instance of this occurred in his tenth year. Henry had taken a walk alone, and had crossed a suspension bridge, paying a small copper coin as the toll. Returning, he found that he needed a second coin to get back across—and he had spent his last bit of money!

While the boy pondered what to do, an old man approached the bridge. Henry promptly approached him.

"Will you lend me a sou?" he asked boldly. "I am Henry Layard. Everyone knows me."

The old man was startled by Henry's self-assurance, and gave him the coin, asking the boy his address. Later, he called on the Layards, told Henry's father about the episode, and, grinning over the boy's impudence, said, "He will go far in the world!"

The Layards continued to move from place to place. France did not suit Henry Peter Layard's delicate constitution, and Switzerland proved equally unsuitable. So it was back to Florence once again, where the elder Layard had had little difficulty with his asthma.

The wanderers settled in the fifteenth-century palace of a noble Florentine family, the Rucellai, who were reduced to poverty and forced to rent out part of their mansion. Henry played with the young Rucellai, who lived on a higher floor of the palace, and had the run of the house.

At school in Florence, Layard learned Italian, but little else. He was still a stubborn, independent-minded boy, and, as in France, he was the only Protestant among a group of Catholics. He shirked his wearisome studies and spent his time hunting butterflies on the nearby hills.

Now he became a hungry reader. Walter Scott and *The Arabian Nights* filled him with feverish excitement. Henry dreamed of visiting the scenes of Scheherazade's stories—and also, inspired by the masterpieces of art with which Florence abounded, he asked his father to let him be trained as a painter. Young Henry did study with several Florentine artists, but not on a serious scale, because his father had other—and more prosaic—plans for him.

Henry was destined to be a lawyer. His uncle, Benjamin Austen, was a respected and prosperous solicitor, and Henry was due to go to him as an articled clerk, with the hope someday of entering the Austen firm as a partner.

Mr. Austen visited the Layards in Florence and saw the life Henry was leading—dreaming away the hours with *The Arabian Nights* or roaming the endless galleries of Florence's two greatest museums, the Uffizi and the Pitti.

"It won't do," Benjamin Austen said flatly. "What sort of training is this for the law? Put the boy in a decent English school or he'll come to nothing."

The elder Layard yielded. He agreed to take Henry back to England. To his great grief Henry found himself leaving Florence again, in the spring of 1829, just after his twelfth birthday.

England's bleak and chilly atmosphere held little promise for him. As usual, he had trouble with his schoolmates—this time because he was a "foreigner," his head full of French and Italian. "I found myself among seventy or eighty boys," he says, "who had been brought up differently from myself. We had little or nothing in common. I had tastes which seemed repugnant to them, and my head was crammed full of things and ideas which they despised."

One of the first questions he was asked was, "What do you know?"

"French and Italian," Henry replied.

"Take that, then," was the response, and a kick and a cuff followed to show contempt for his accomplishments.

He continued to find companionship in the world of books. He read works of travel in the Near East and historical novels, and even serious works of history such as Gibbons' *Decline and Fall*. He started to think he could become a novelist himself and "actually commenced a romance . . . opening with the customary knight, clad in armor, wending his weary way, as the sun went down, through a romantic valley. But I never got beyond the first chapter or two."

Ahead of him lay a cheerless prospect: his career as a lawyer. He was made to read ponderous law tomes such as Blackstone's *Commentaries*, which he found hard going, slipping back to a book of travels whenever no one watched him. In 1834, the seventeen-year-old Layard became a clerk for his uncle's firm, and to satisfy Benjamin Austen's vanity juggled his name around to place "Austen" first. But everyone always continued to call him "Henry."

The drudgery of his new job appalled him. Living alone in a back room of a London boarding house, he was supposed to spend most of his waking hours carrying out routine clerical tasks for his uncle, and the rest of them studying textbooks of law. Dutifully, he did his best, but law held no fascination for him. He took up playing the flute for relaxation, read books of adventure, and did everything possible to avoid having to dip into the hated legal volumes.

For five dreary years Layard plugged away at law. He met many notable figures of the time at his uncle's offices —members of Parliament, cabinet officials, even some noblemen. One of the frequent visitors at the Austens was a strange, foppish young man named Benjamin Disraeli, who, Layard tells us, "wore waistcoats of the most gorgeous colors and the most fantastic patterns, with much gold embroidery, velvet pantaloons, and shoes adorned with red rosettes. I thought him conceited and unkind because he would not answer the questions about his Eastern travels which I had the impertinence to put to him."

Disraeli's travels in the Near East were not the only

source of his appeal for Layard. He was a novelist, who had had some of his works actually published! And he had political ambitions. He would walk up and down the room, declaring, "When I am Prime Minister, I shall do so and so." Striking the mantel violently with his fist, Disraeli would insist, "Laugh as you may, I *shall* be Prime Minister!"

Soon Disraeli was a member of Parliament, and no longer was seen at the Austens. Many years passed before Layard would meet him again—and, of course, Disraeli *did* become Prime Minister, in 1868. His political path and Layard's often crossed in later years.

Layard forced himself grimly to go on with his law studies. His father, meanwhile, had settled in the country town of Aylesbury. Despite his poor health, he felt it necessary to remain in England to supervise the education of his four sons. His asthma grew rapidly worse, and he died in October 1834. Young Henry Layard became head of his family at seventeen and a half.

His own health was showing signs of weakening under the strain of his studies. At a doctor's suggestion, Layard went abroad for a long trip through the Alps in the summer of 1835. He traveled with a painter, William Brockeden. It was the first of Layard's many trips as an adult. The wanderings of his childhood had left him with a taste for travel, which he proceeded to satisfy temporarily now. In the summers that followed, he continued to go abroad. But always it was back to the doleful study of law when the fair weather came to an end.

It was soon apparent enough to Benjamin Austen that his nephew was not going to make a very good lawyer. Young Layard had no interest in law, no visible liking for it, no abilities of a legal kind. Layard came to the uncomfortable realization that he had wasted his time; that there was not going to be any room for him in the Austen firm.

How, then, was he going to earn a living?

He was troubled and unsettled, floundering at loose ends. Then there came upon the scene his uncle, Charles Layard, younger brother of Henry Peter Layard, who had settled in Ceylon more than thirty years before. Now he was visiting England, and he swiftly learned that his brother's oldest son was in difficulties over his profession.

"Come to Ceylon," Uncle Charles proposed. "You can be a lawyer there. The island is flourishing. If you fail at the law, you can always open a coffee plantation."

It was a tempting idea. Ceylon held the lure of the exotic, the magnetism of the Orient. If he went there, Layard would at least escape the drabness of England.

Going to his other uncle, Benjamin Austen, Layard let it be known that he planned to head eastward. "He was sincerely grieved at learning it," Layard noted—but Austen was also probably a little relieved to have the problem of his untalented nephew taken from him.

In June 1839 Layard took his law examinations, and somehow managed to pass them. He was enrolled as an attorney and solicitor of Her Majesty's Courts, with the right to practice law in Ceylon. "The examination was not, perhaps, a very severe one," Layard remarked. But it did require at least a sketchy knowledge of the law, and that much he had.

His mother held a certain sum of money in trust for her sons, amounting to £600—then about $3000—apiece. She turned £300 of this immediately over to her son, to cover his expenses on his journey to Ceylon, and the other half was sent directly ahead to that island to be held by Charles Layard until Henry arrived.

Ceylon beckoned. Austen Henry Layard set out on his eastward journey. He never would, as it happened, get to Ceylon. Destiny would sidetrack him, and he would spend the next eight and a half years in Turkey, Persia and other lands of the Orient. When next he returned to England, he would be neither a lawyer nor a coffee-planter, but "Nineveh" Layard, the famed explorer and archaeologist.

II

THE LONG WAY TO CEYLON

Travel nowadays is a streamlined operation. If a young London solicitor today had business in Ceylon, he would board a jet airliner, eat a meal, and descend, only a few hours later, at his destination. The whole process poses hardly any problems at all.

It was not quite so elementary in 1839. A journey to Ceylon meant a voyage at sea lasting many months and exposing the traveler to danger and hardship—or a voyage overland lasting perhaps twice as long, taking the traveler through parts of the world hardly better known to Europeans of that time than the surface of the moon is to us. The hardships meant nothing to Henry Layard, however. His brain teemed with colorful memories of *The Arabian Nights,* and he knew that en route to Ceylon he would have a chance to pass through fabled Constantinople and storied Baghdad, he would be able to see all the glittering cities of the Near East with his own eyes.

For that reason, he had no intentions of journeying by sea. The overland trek it would be! He quickly found a traveling companion who shared his tastes—Edward Ledwich Mitford, a young Englishman who had spent some time in North Africa and who now planned to go to Ceylon as a coffee-planter. Mitford disliked travel by sea. Charles Layard introduced him to his nephew, and they soon had their itinerary worked out.

They agreed to travel together, as far as possible by land. They would proceed through Central Europe, passing through Dalmatia and Montenegro (now parts of Yugoslavia), Albania and Bulgaria, to Constantinople.

Constantinople was then the capital of Turkey, and the Turkish Empire of 1839 was a vastly different entity from the Turkey of today. Then, Turkey sprawled out over much of the Near East. Egypt, Syria, Palestine, Lebanon, Iraq—all were Turkish provinces. And Turkey also extended far into Europe, ruling much of the Balkan region and even part of Greece. Constantinople, then, was one of the most important cities in the world, center of a vast empire.

From Constantinople, Layard and Mitford planned to cross Asia Minor to Syria and Palestine, and to explore the Holy Land. From there, they would strike northward across the Mesopotamian desert to Baghdad, and turn eastward again through Persia and Afghanistan, and then down through India to Ceylon.

It was an ambitious plan—so ambitious that Layard's family thought it was insane, and a respected friend of Henry's told him he was embarking on "a wild-goose chase." Nothing could shake him. His imagination was inflamed by the idea of visiting Aleppo, Damascus, Baghdad and Isfahan, whose names figure so often in *The Arabian Nights*. He had read the works of almost every traveler who had visited that part of the world. His mind was fevered with dreams of Persia and Babylonia.

Then, too, he was happy to bid England farewell. He saw no future for himself there. The English were stern, puritanical folk, and Layard, raised in France and Italy, did not find them congenial. He disliked the idea of practicing law in England. And his political opinions were unpopular ones—he was liberal and independent, always championing the weak and the poor. At that time, the Conservative

Party, the Tories, dominated England, and anyone who did not share Tory ideas was looked upon by "decent people" as a rabble-rouser.

Layard and Mitford expected their journey to take them about a year. Since neither one was a man of means, they planned to travel as cheaply as possible, taking no servant along, hiring no guides, and finding their own way with the aid of a compass. They were aware that the journey would be dangerous, but brushed aside all fears. Layard was too young, too robust, and too optimistic to worry much about such things, and Mitford, an experienced traveler, felt capable of surmounting any obstacles.

One of these obstacles was the fact that England and Persia had just broken off diplomatic relations, and were on the verge of going to war. Two unescorted Englishmen would hardly be welcome in Persia at such a time.

The former British Ambassador to Persia, Sir John MacNeill, had returned to London. Layard and Mitford sought him out and asked him how they should travel in Persia.

"You must either travel as important personages," he told them, "with a retinue of servants and an adequate escort, or else alone, as poor men, with nothing to excite the greed of the people among whom you will have to mix."

The two travelers prepared carefully for their risky trip. Layard studied some Arabic and Persian. He took lessons in surveying, so he would have at least a rough idea of his general location most of the time. A retired sea captain taught him how to use the sextant, how to take observations of the sun to find latitude, how to fix the positions of mountain peaks to give locations.

He provided himself with a pocket sextant and some other surveying equipment, a compass, a barometer, some thermometers, and a good silver watch, which on the advice of an experienced traveler he painted black, so the sight of the gleaming metal would not arouse the greed of the wild tribesmen he would encounter.

Since they would have to be their own doctors, Layard visited a doctor who gave him a quick course in medicine, teaching him the symptoms of those diseases he was likely to be exposed to, such as dysentery, ophthalmia and intermittent fever, showing him how to bandage wounds, how to use a tourniquet and how to lance boils. He gave Layard a medicine kit that proved invaluable to him abroad.

They traveled with a minimum of belongings—only enough clothing and possessions to fill one saddlebag apiece. Since they planned to wear native clothing when abroad, they could add to their wardrobes as they went. Layard allowed himself one luxury: "what was called a 'Levinge bed'—a pair of sheets sewn together and attached to a mosquito curtain, forming a kind of bag, which, when closed (the curtain being attached to a nail in the wall), formed a complete defense against insects of all kinds, whether crawling, hopping, or flying, that abound in the dirty houses . . . that we were warned we should have to occupy . . . in the East."

For all his boldness and confidence, Layard felt just a twinge of doubt as he and Mitford left England, on July 8, 1839. His future was unknown. His chances of success in Ceylon were uncertain. His plans were vague and somewhat wild. If he failed in this new venture, what would become of him?

He shrugged his fears away. He was twenty-two, healthy, independent. He had a little money, enough to see him through his trip. He no longer needed to hearken to the voices of his relatives. He did not have to behave after the approved fashions of society. He could go where he pleased, do as he pleased, and he felt that he had courage and determination enough to grapple with any dangers and difficulties he might meet. His only regret in leaving England was at parting with his mother.

Crossing the English Channel, Layard and Mitford landed at Ostend and spent a few days exploring the museums and monuments of Belgium before starting eastward. Traveling in the cheapest available way at all times, they passed through Germany and Italy, missing hardly any important cathedral or art collection as they went.

Venice marked the easternmost boundary of "civilized" Europe in those days. Beyond lay rough, half-wild country. Eastern Europe was largely in Turkish hands, and the people were peasants, many of them Moslems. So there was an element of risk in passing through Dalmatia and Montenegro and points east.

But not until they crossed from Montenegro into Albania did they actually reach Turkish soil. At last Layard had entered the Orient, the world of which he had dreamed from childhood. He was not disappointed. He tells us:

"The scene around me was so strange and new, I could scarcely follow our guide. The booths in the covered alleys of the bazaar, the endless variety of merchandise piled up in them, the embroideries and strange dresses that were suspended around them, the grave Turk sitting cross-legged amidst his stores, pipe in hand, the veiled women gliding through the crowd, the jaunty Albanian with his . . . long gun resplendent with coral and silver, his richly inlaid pistols, the savory messes steaming in the cooks' shops, and the dim and mysterious light of the place, through which all this was seen, greatly increased the effect that it could not fail to make on me."

They continued onward into Turkish Bulgaria. While sleeping in a drafty shack in a marshy plain near Philippopolis (Plovdiv), Layard developed gastritis, and by the time he and Mitford reached Constantinople he was delirious with fever and had to take to bed. He was given over to the care of one Dr. Z., "an Armenian gentleman who had studied medicine at Edinburgh." Layard remarks, "He bled me twice copiously, and, moreover, made a large circle with a pen and ink on my stomach, which he offered to be filled with leeches." The loss of blood through this then-approved "healing" method so weakened Layard that he was out of commission for three weeks, leaving Mitford to explore the Turkish capital alone.

On October 4 they were ready to resume their journey. For the equivalent of $125 they bought three horses, one apiece to ride and a third for luggage, and hired a Greek named Giorgio, who claimed to speak Italian, French, Turkish and Arabic, to serve for a while as their guide and cook.

Turkey was then in a state of chaos. The Sultan had died in July, and his successor had not yet established full control over the whole vast empire. The Egyptian governor, Mohammed Ali, was in open revolt against the Turks. Egyptian troops under Mohammed Ali's son, Ibrahim Pasha, had defeated a Turkish army in Syria, and the scattered Turkish soldiers were running wild in Asia Minor, plundering and looting to console themselves for their defeat.

Into this confusion went Layard and Mitford— neither of them able to speak a word of Turkish, knowing almost nothing about the country they were entering, and carrying maps that were so imperfect as to be almost useless. In the European provinces of Turkey they had met with politeness and courtesy everywhere—but what fate was in store as they moved eastward?

They struck out for the heart of Asia Minor, deliberately choosing a route no European travelers had taken before, through mountains and forests to the Mediterranean coast. The map they carried showed only a blank here, and they had to trust to their compass, to Giorgio's knowledge, and to whatever information they could pick up as they moved from village to village.

Layard quickly found that getting information from Turks was no easy matter. They had a violent dislike for giving straight answers. One day, meeting a shepherd driving his flock, Layard asked him how many goats he had.

"As many as passed by you," the shepherd said.

"But I didn't count them. How many are there?"

"The same number I took with me to the mountains."

"But how many did you take to the mountains?"

"As many as I had."

It was just as futile with the driver of a caravan of laden camels. Asking him where he had come from, Layard was answered with a pointed finger: "From that side."

"But from what town?" the perplexed Englishman wanted to know.

"The town is there."

"But the *name* of the town?"

An evasive shrug. "It was towards Smyrna."

Despite these difficulties, Layard and Mitford proceeded steadily onward. They found the inhabitants less friendly as they went, and when they reached the town of Konia they got their first taste of the sort of Oriental treatment that was going to become woefully familiar before long.

The people of Konia had never seen Europeans before,

and were suspicious of them. The chief of the village demanded their papers, and shook his head stubbornly when Layard produced his *firman*, or permit from the Sultan to travel in Turkey.

"It is not in order," the chief declared flatly. "You cannot go further. You must go back where you came."

Layard knew well enough that his *firman* was acceptable, and that the chief was simply being troublesome. Taking out his watch, Layard said, "Unless we are allowed to go on our way in ten minutes, I will file a formal complaint with the Sultan against you for disobedience to the Sultan's orders and contempt for the Imperial *firman*."

The chief held a hasty meeting with his council, none of whom could actually read the *firman*, and it was finally decided to let the travelers continue. Returning to the inn where they had left their baggage during the interview, the Englishmen found another melancholy surprise awaiting them: the *odabashi*, or innkeeper, had gone through their things and helped himself to their money and some of their goods!

Seizing the culprit, Layard dragged him back to the chief—who, thoroughly cowed now by these arrogant Englishmen, ordered the return of everything that had been stolen. The matter was closed, and the travelers departed —having had a good baptism in Oriental red tape and Oriental thievery as well.

They completed the crossing of Asia Minor without further serious incident, visiting many interesting Greek and Phoenician ruins as they went. Layard found himself regretting the incompleteness of his early education: "Neither my companion or myself had sufficiently prepared ourselves for exploring regions so rich in classic and historic associations, and so full of objects probably new to science.

I had turned my attention but little to archaeology, and I had but a mere smattering of scientific knowledge of any kind."

But the firsthand experience of traveling through Turkey had been invaluable. He had seen much, and he had passed happy and delightful days, the toil and privations notwithstanding. And above all he enjoyed his independence.

They were now about to enter Syria—which meant departing from the Sultan's domain, and entering territory held by the rebellious Egyptians. The Sultan's *firman* would do them no good here, and they would have to trust for their safety to the fact that they were Englishmen.

Now, at last, Layard was in true *Arabian Nights* country. Southward they journeyed through the Levant, through cities rich with thousands of years of colorful history— Tarsus, Antioch, Aleppo. In Aleppo, Layard came down with a recurrence of his intermittent fever, and—having been taught the trick in Constantinople—bled himself by applying leeches. Then it was onward into what is now Lebanon—Beirut, Tripoli, Gebeil. In the hills above Beirut he carved his name on the bark of a Cedar of Lebanon that may have been old when the Assyrian kings were building the palaces of Nineveh. Their servant Giorgio, tired of wandering, resigned from their services there, and they did not replace him.

Onward, ever southward—to the ancient Phoenician cities, still very much alive and bustling, of Tyre and Sidon. At Tyre, on the first day of January 1840, they met a French painter, Horace Vernet, who had come to the Levant to paint military scenes of the battles between the Egyptians and the Turks.

Vernet was equipped with an unusual gadget, which Layard examined in wonder. It was a Daguerrotype, the first camera, invented in France only a few months before. Layard was awed as Vernet photographed the monuments and scenes of Tyre with the unwieldy instrument.

The next day, Layard and Mitford saddled up and rode southward, into the hilly country of Judea. For nearly a week they plodded through stony, barren hills, broken only by an occasional terrace planted with olive and fig trees. There were few living creatures to be seen. The Egyptians, ruling oppressively, had taxed the natives so heavily that nearly everyone had fled. Layard was amused to discover that those villages still under Turkish rule cried out to be "liberated" by the Egyptians, while those that had been captured by the rebellious Egyptians begged for the return of the Turks!

On January 9, 1840, they reached Jerusalem, and paused to plan the next stage of their journey. Layard wanted to visit Petra, Ammon, and the other ruined cities in the desert east of the Jordan. Mitford pointed out that it was mid-winter, the rainy season, and they would have no shelter from the elements. Besides, the desert was held by Arab tribes who preyed mercilessly on all travelers.

Layard insisted on going. In a friendly way, the voyagers agreed to separate. Layard would make his journey through the desert alone, circling around the Dead Sea and doubling back northward to Aleppo, where he would rejoin Mitford for the trip to Baghdad.

The English Consul in Jerusalem was aghast when he heard Layard's plan. "I refuse to take any responsibility for what may happen to you," he said bluntly. "It's suicide to go into that desert alone."

He told Layard that the Arab sheikhs recognized no

authority but their own, and were constantly at war with one another. He surely would be murdered, or at least robbed of all he possessed, if he attempted the journey.

Such warnings only served to spur Layard onward. Although he now knew some Arabic, he decided to take an interpreter with him, and found an Arab boy of nineteen who had been converted to Christianity and who now bore the name Antonio. Antonio had a smattering of French and Italian, and so would be able to communicate with Layard and with any Arab chieftains they met in the desert. On January 15, Layard and Antonio set out into the barren, bandit-infested wastes beyond Jerusalem.

Layard had a strategy for dealing with the Arabs. He knew that hospitality was sacred among Arab wanderers of the desert—even the most murderous ones. If, therefore, you could enter an Arab camp and claim the rights of a guest, you were safe. The Arabs would willingly offer food and shelter, for which payment would be a deadly insult, and from then on you would be under their protection. On the other hand, if they came upon you unawares, no obligation of hospitality would exist, and they were free to plunder or kill as they pleased.

Layard's tactic was to avoid discovery until he was upon an Arab encampment, then boldly to enter and beg accommodation. It worked, after a fashion—which is to say that he survived the trip. But not all the Arabs practiced their ancient customs of hospitality with equal warmth. Some tried to extort "presents" of cash or possessions from the Englishman. Others slyly went through his saddlebag when he slept, forcing him to make ugly scenes in the morning in order to regain his property. It was a harrowing and constantly dangerous journey, and he was plagued and troubled by the different Arab tribes in every way conceivable.

None of this harsh treatment could dampen his spirits, neither robbery nor extortion nor the threat of death itself. He ran new risks every few miles, when he would come into the territory of some new sheikh, and had to repeat the same tiresome business of introducing himself and fending off Arab trickery, thievery and extortion attempts.

Layard stopped each night at a different Arab encampment. The Arabs, who wandered nomadically through the desert, would set up each day black goatskin tents, forming an enclosure in which the tribe's sheep and lambs were penned. Bonfires lit the scene. The Arabs dined on rice and boiled mutton, dipping their fingers into wooden bowls. Their hospitality was usually generous—though Layard knew he was never really safe.

The most important of the ruins he visited on this trip was the city of Petra, a striking city cut into the rock of great limestone cliffs. Many travelers have gone into raptures over Petra, the "rose-red city half as old as time." Layard, independent as always, was moved by the extreme desolation and savage character of the scene, but was bold enough to dismiss the city itself by saying, "I thought the architecture debased and wanting both in elegance and grandeur. It is of a bad period and a corrupt style."

There were other ruins ahead. Layard forged tirelessly toward them, undismayed by lurking Arabs who sometimes descended from the hills to try to rob him.

A typical Layard adventure occurred near the Dead Sea, as he was bound for the town of Kerak. He had picked up along the way an Arab named Awad to guide him through this part of the desert. One morning, a second Arab joined them. Awad recognized him as Mahmoud, sheikh of a small tribe nearby. Several of Mahmoud's followers skulked a short distance away.

Busying himself with breakfast, Layard looked up and found Awad and Mahmoud struggling for possession of his saddlebags. Through Antonio, Layard demanded to know what was going on.

"The sheikh says," Antonio faltered, "that unless you pay him much money for passing through his tribe, you will be robbed and murdered."

Layard had already learned that the best way to deal with these Arabs was the bold way. He drew his gun and leveled it at Mahmoud's head, and announced that he would keep the sheikh as hostage for his safe conduct through the area.

"Disarm him," he ordered, and Antonio took Mahmoud's knife, his pistol, and his club. Layard proceeded to sit down and enjoy his scanty breakfast of boiled rice and bread, and even invited his prisoner to share his meal.

After breakfast, the entourage moved on toward Kerak, Mahmoud in tow. Suddenly a pair of spear-carrying Arabs came running down the slope. They were two of the followers of Mahmoud, who had vanished when their sheikh was captured.

"Order them to go back," Layard told Mahmoud.

The Arabs continued to approach. One drew near and saluted, while the other crept up and snatched away Layard's cloak, which had been resting on his pack-saddle.

"This first theft," Layard writes, "was the signal for a general attack upon my property. Arabs appeared, as if by magic, from above and below. I dragged Mahmoud, whom I had seized by the arm, toward the camels. Thinking that I intended to shoot him, he entreated the robbers, who had almost surrounded me, to draw back. Seeing the danger to which their sheikh was exposed, they hesitated to fall upon me."

At this point yet another Arab sheikh arrived and attempted to put a stop to the quarrel. He knew Awad, who explained to him that Layard "was travelling under the protection of Abu-Dhaouk, who was responsible to Ibrahim Pasha for my safety, and that I had letters for the Mujelli, or governor, of Kerak, who would also be answerable to the Egyptian Government should any injury befall me."

This complicated explanation brought about a stop to hostilities. The peacemaking sheikh, though, asked Layard to yield up his gun, which he refused to do. While the matter was under discussion, a ferocious Arab named Beshire suddenly leaped on Awad, and seized *his* gun. Awad grabbed it back, and a struggle followed. In the confusion, Mahmoud broke loose from Layard's grasp, but the traveler seized him again.

Now the action resumed. Layard tells us, "The Arabs began throwing stones, and Beshire, who had not succeeded in wresting the gun from Awad, threw his spear at me. Fortunately it glanced by me. My assailants again drew their swords, and one or two fired their pistols at me; but they were too far away to reach me. I exerted myself with all my might to drag Sheikh Mahmoud towards Kerak, menacing him with death when he attempted to stop."

Layard's camels, bothered by the noise and confusion, began to wander away. Some Arabs followed them, and began to loot Layard's belongings. The others, afraid they would lose their share of their booty, joined their companions instead of pursuing Layard. He could see them, as he hurried on with the sheikh, dividing the contents of his saddlebags and other property.

Antonio had fled, and was calling to Layard to follow him, but Layard clung to Sheikh Mahmoud and hurried him along to a nearby encampment of yet another Arab tribe. Layard found the sheikh of this tribe and showed him his letter to the governor of Kerak. The sheikh congratulated Layard on his escape from Mahmoud's men, who were "the most notorious robbers and cutthroats to the east of the Dead Sea."

Ahmen, son of this sheikh, accompanied Layard back to Mahmoud's encampment and made a speech to the Arabs, accusing them of violating the desert code by attacking a man who had eaten bread with their chief. At length, the unruly Arabs grumblingly restored everything they had taken from Layard, his precious maps and notebook, his clothes, his portable tent, everything but a shirt and a pair of trousers, which had already been cut down to fit some naked Arab children.

Layard expressed his gratitude to Ahmed for helping him recover his goods. It was not long, though, before Ahmed himself demanded a reward other than gratitude. "He began by begging for money, which I refused to give him. He then suggested that I might make him a present of my gun, and on my telling him that I would not part with it, asked for my pistols instead. Being still unsuccessful he wanted my sword, then my carpet, and, lastly, my cloak."

They quarreled all day, until Ahmed finally withdrew his demands. Then, and only then, did Layard voluntarily give him the present of his sword, and his tent. He had intended to make some gift to the sheikh's son all along, but resented the attempt at extortion.

And so Layard recovered his property and continued on his way—on toward his next adventure and his next taste of Arab slyness. Modern travelers, with their paid-in-advance tours and their air-conditioned buses, have a drab time of it in comparison with Layard's lively journey!

III

Layard moved steadily northward, eluding the grasp of greedy Arabs as a matter of daily routine. Soon he found himself approaching the great city of Damascus.

There was a new problem now. The desert through which he had been wandering was troubled by plague. For their own safety, the rulers of Damascus had closed the frontier and were allowing no one to enter the city from the plague area. Consulting a Jewish peddler he met on the way, Layard found that his best chance of slipping past the blockade was to travel on into the desert and come onto Damascus from the north. But this meant a delay of five or six days, and Mitford, waiting for him in Aleppo, was likely to grow impatient and perhaps depart without him.

Layard decided to try his luck on a direct approach, and continued straight for Damascus. He stopped for the night at an inn a few days' journey away, and was himself exposed to the plague, since the inn had only one room, and everyone slept on the floor in a huddle. "The room," he writes, "was filled with villagers during the greater part of the night. Many of them had been in contact during the day with persons who were dying, or had died, of the plague. Some were perhaps already infected with the fatal disease, and were shortly to be its victims."

To make things worse, in the morning the villagers began bringing plague victims to him to be cured. "For it is well known," one villager told him, "that all Franks [Europeans] are healers and men of medicine."

Layard was no doctor, and such medicines as he carried were useful only for fevers and colds. He made his excuses, and quickly resumed his journey, leaving the plague city behind as fast as he could.

As he drew nearer to Damascus, he was set upon again —not by Arabs, this time, but by deserters from the Egyptian army. They were armed with guns, and resistance was useless. They tore off Layard's money-belt, containing a few gold coins, and demanded and received his supply of tobacco as well. But they left him with the things he really valued—his gun, his compass, his watch, his medicines, and his books and papers.

He camped for the night on a hill overlooking Damascus, shivering in a drenching downpour, and in the middle of the night, guided by an Arab who claimed he was an experienced blockade-runner, proceeded to enter the city in pitch blackness. Layard stumbled along, sore-footed, over rocks and gravel, climbing walls and fences. "The rain continued to descend in torrents. He [the guide] went steadily on his way, wading through swollen rivulets and deep mud, scrambling over rocks, and creeping through ditches and watercourses. I followed him silently, making as little noise as possible. We walked for some hours, occasionally stopping for a few minutes, as I was nearly exhausted. When the day broke we could see the gardens of Damascus within a short distance of us."

Layard was past the blockade—but no sooner had he entered the city than a policeman galloped up, and had to be bribed with gold before he would let the ragged, dirty wanderer proceed. Passing into Damascus proper, Layard made his way through numberless winding streets, enclosed by the mud-built walls of houses, to the British Consulate.

The British Consul was astonished at the young traveller's appearance—"clad in scarcely more than a tattered cloak, almost shoeless, and bronzed and begrimed by long exposure to sun and weather and to the dirt of Arab tents." A hot bath and a suit of fresh clothes transformed Layard into something more English-looking. The Consul told him that Mitford had been there, and had gone on toward Aleppo as arranged.

Layard departed in a few days, stopping to visit the famed ruins of Baalbek, and running into the usual difficulties with rapacious natives on the way. He also got his first view of Assyrian sculptures carved on the face of a rock at Nahr-el-Kelb (he mistakenly thought they were Phoenician, but was able to identify them properly later, when he was an expert on Assyrian art).

Mitford was waiting none too patiently for him in Aleppo, and indeed had been about to go on to Baghdad alone. "He consented to remain there for a few days more," Layard notes, "to give me and my mare a little rest, of which we were both very much in need. On March 18 we left Aleppo together." Layard had been traveling alone for two months—but it must have seemed like as many years to him.

They struck northward, now, and re-entered Turkish lands as they approached the Mesopotamian desert. Layard and Mitford approached Baghdad in their usual roundabout way, by going far to the north, all the way to Mosul, and then swinging southward again along the Tigris.

They reached Mosul on April 10, 1840. "The town, with its walls and minarets and gardens, stretching along the right bank of the Tigris, has the appearance of a considerable city. It was only when we entered it that we realized the condition of ruin and decay to which it had been reduced by long misgovernment and neglect."

And now Layard got his first glimpse of the mounds at Mosul that would occupy him so intensely in the years to come. He wrote of seeing "stern shapeless mounds rising like a hill from the scorched plain. . . . Desolation meets desolation; a feeling of awe succeeds to wonder; for there is nothing to relieve the mind, to lead to hope, or to tell of what has gone by."

Those ugly heaps of earth had been great cities once. Thousands of years ago, thriving civilizations had lived in the then-fertile plains surrounding the Tigris and Euphrates —the oldest civilizations in the world, perhaps. The area was already unimaginably ancient when the Greeks began to call it Mesopotamia—"The Land between the Two Rivers."

A shrewd and inventive people called the Sumerians had built the first great cities of Mesopotamia, about six thousand years ago. They built canals and reservoirs, wrote poetry, knew the arts of music and medicine. For thousands of years the Sumerians were masters of their part of the world. But then barbarian invaders came out of the west. A king named Sargon, ruling a tribe speaking a language of the family we call Semitic, conquered the great cities of Sumer and welded them into his own empire.

Sargon's mighty empire gave way in its turn. Out of centuries of chaos in Mesopotamia there came two new kingdoms, finally, about 1800 B.C. In the south, the flat, hot land that had once been Sumer was now Babylonia, whose first great king was Hammurabi the Lawgiver. Babylonia embraced most of the old Sumerian cities, such as Ur and Nippur and Lagash, and also included the new Semitic cities, such as Babylon. The Babylonians continued most of the traditions of the Sumerians.

In the north, where the land was more mountainous

and the climate harsher—hot in summer, chill and rainy in winter—sprang up the kingdom of Assyria, whose capital was the great city of Nineveh. The Assyrians spoke the same language as the Babylonians and were of the same racial stock. But they were quite different in their culture.

The Assyrians were warlike and brutal. They had little culture of their own. Whatever they had in the way of poetry, art or religion was taken over from the Babylonians —who, in turn, had adapted it from the Sumerians. For hundreds of years, Assyria was an insignificant nation whose small cities spent their energies in attacking one another. Babylonia was supreme in Mesopotamia.

About 1600 B.C., tough mountaineers conquered Babylonia, and ruled it for the next 450 years. During those years, the Assyrians in the north gradually gathered strength. The Babylonians freed themselves only to find the Assyrians on the warpath.

Assyria conquered Babylonia about 1100 B.C. Then the sinister hordes of Assyria raged throughout the Near East, looting and pillaging and destroying. The world trembled at the might of the Assyrian. But, in time, destruction came even to grim Assyria.

Her cities were burned by jubilant enemies. Her lands were divided. Assyria's charred splendors vanished from sight, became grass-covered mounds that studded the Mesopotamian landscape. They were not forgotten—not entirely. Vague local tradition still held that one mound, near the modern city of Baghdad, was old Babylon, and that another mound, far to the north near Mosul, was fabled Nineveh. But these stories were unreliable and legend-shrouded. For hundreds of years, no one investigated those mounds. For hundreds of years, the lost cities of Assyria and Babylonia slumbered.

Now Henry Layard, his mind full of *Arabian Nights* legends, had reached Mosul, and looked upon those mounds, "deeply moved," as he writes, "by their desolate and solitary grandeur."

Layard, always the romantic, was eager to believe that the mounds at Mosul really did contain the ruins of Nineveh. Indeed, he refused to think they might be anything else. He felt certain that beneath these grassy heaps lay the remains of the Assyrian cities, and he was seized with the passionate desire to dig into them. But he had neither the time nor money to excavate. That would have to wait.

Standing by the mounds of Mosul, Layard found his imagination taking him back to the days when the foot of the Assyrian bestrode the neck of the world, and the proud cities of Assyria glittered with treasure. He knew the stories of the Old Testament, telling of the deeds of the grim Assyrian rulers, the harsh, alien crackle of whose names runs through the pages of Isaiah and Ezekiel and Jeremiah. Tiglath-Pileser and Sargon and Shalmaneser and Sennacherib —names to conjure with! Mighty kings, who built mighty cities—Assur and Calah, Dur-Sharrukin and Nineveh.

Nineveh!

Here, Layard knew, *must* be Nineveh! That hotbed of sin, that rich, arrogant, wicked city—it was here. He remembered the Biblical story, how the Lord sent the prophet Jonah to preach to the Ninevites, telling him, "Arise, go to Nineveh, that great city, and cry against it; for their wickedness is come up before me." Jonah disobeyed the heavenly commandment, and fled, only to be swallowed up by a great fish, and when he came forth he finally did carry the word of God to Nineveh.

The Ninevites repented of their sins, said the Bible, but their repentance soon was forgotten. Soon they were back at their sinful ways. And here was the visible evidence of the wages of sin.

Through Layard's mind rolled the words of Lord Byron's poem, *The Destruction of Sennacherib*:

The Assyrian came down like the wolf on the fold,
And his cohorts were gleaming in purple and gold;
And the sheen of their spears was like stars on the sea,
When the blue wave rolls nightly on deep Galilee.

And what was left of mighty Nineveh? Layard looked, and saw desolation. "Fragments of pottery," he wrote, "and the stupendous mass of brickwork occasionally laid bare by the winter rains." The ruins of palaces, buried by shifting desert sand. The shattered glory of a lost civilization.

In Mosul, Layard met another English adventurer named Ainsworth, who had also shown some interest in the supposed Nineveh mounds. Ainsworth introduced him to a Christian native of the city, Christian Rassam, who had recently been appointed British Vice-Consul. Layard also met the Vice-Consul's half-brother, Hormuzd Rassam. These three men took Layard for his first visit to the buried ruins of Nineveh.

He spent a week among the mounds, measuring them and searching for fragments of inscriptions and statuary, and wishing that he had the money to hire workmen and clear away the earth. Layard was not the first to feel the excitement of the Mesopotamian mounds, of course. Other European travelers since the beginning of the nineteenth century had seen them and examined them, and Layard, of course, had read their books with the keenest fascination.

One of the first Europeans to study the mounds had

been a brilliant young man named Claudius Rich, who had mastered most of the languages of the Orient while still in his teens, and who had won the important post of representative of the British East India Company at Baghdad. Rich, in 1811, first visited the mounds near Baghdad, which supposedly marked the site of Babylon. He did not dig, but he explored the surface of a mound still called Babel, at the modern town of Hillah, and discovered bricks, engraved stones, fragments of inscriptions and wooden coffins. He drew a careful map of the ruins, and wrote a book about his discoveries.

Rich next journeyed northward, in 1820, to Mosul. Huge mounds rose across the Tigris, on the bank opposite the city, and the locals told him, "That is where Nineveh was!" Rich's curiosity was further excited by reports that a sculpture, showing men and animals, had been dug up not long before in one part of the mound. All of Mosul had come to view the wonderful sculpture. One of the city's religious leaders, unfortunately, had denounced it as a work of infidels—and the Moslems of Mosul, having been warned in the Koran of Mohammed to spurn all idols, had obediently destroyed it.

Rich examined several of the mounds about Mosul. The first was Nebbi Yunus, which was supposed to be the site of the tomb of the prophet Jonah. There, he found a few inscribed stones, and under the mosque containing the tomb itself he was shown passageways leading into the mound. He was not, however, allowed to explore further, since the mound was considered sacred.

Nearby was the largest mound of the group, called Kouyunjik. Probing in the rubble atop the mound, Rich found some bricks stamped with the wedge-shaped cuneiform characters of old Babylonian writing, and some remains of ancient buildings. He surveyed the mound, finding its circumference to be 7690 feet, but he did not attempt to excavate.

"With the exception of a small stone chair and a few remains of inscriptions," Henry Layard wrote thirty years later, "Mr. Rich obtained no other Assyrian relics from the ruins on the site of Nineveh; and he left Mosul, little suspecting that in these mounds were buried the palaces of the Assyrian Kings. As he floated down the Tigris to Baghdad, he landed at Nimroud [another mound, eighteen miles south of Mosul] and examined the great mound. He was struck by its evident antiquity. . . . He obtained a few specimens of bricks bearing cuneiform characters, and proceeded with his journey.

"The fragments collected by Mr. Rich were subsequently placed in the British Museum, and formed the principal, and indeed almost only collection of Assyrian antiquities in Europe. A case scarcely three feet square inclosed all that remained, not only of the great city, Nineveh, but of Babylon itself!"

Rich had never been in good health, and a cholera epidemic took his life the year after his visit to Mosul. His wife edited his manuscripts and presented them for publication. Layard, one of the many who read Rich's books, found them even more exciting than the fantasies of the *Arabian Nights.*

Now, on his first visit to the area, Layard could not get enough of ruins. On April 18, after he had roamed the Mosul mounds as thoroughly as time permitted, Layard was taken by Ainsworth and Christian Rassam into the desert, to view some other ruins to the south. En route, Layard came down with an attack of fever and grew delirious. The party camped at the village of Hammun Ali while he recovered his strength, and that night, as the sun dropped, Layard saw yet another great conical mound outlined against the sky. It was the mound of Nimroud, the ancient city of Calah, where five years later he would make his first great archaeological finds.

The next morning Layard felt better, and the party continued down the Tigris, keeping wary eyes out both for parties of bandits and for the wild lions that still roamed that section of Mesopotamia. At daybreak the following morning, they reached still another towering mound —this one known as Qalah Shergat. They spent the day there, taking measurements and unearthing bits of pottery, bricks and the foundations of buildings.

The bricks were often stamped with odd wedge-shaped characters that looked like nothing so much as chicken-scratches. Layard knew that this was an ancient form of writing, but no one could decipher it. Since the seventeenth century, it had been called *cuneiform* writing, from the Latin word *cuneus*, meaning "wedge."

Though Layard could not possibly have known it, cuneiform writing was even older than the elegant hieroglyphics of Egypt, which had recently been decoded. Cuneiform was the product of the Sumerians, those early inhabitants of Mesopotamia. The invention of writing was the supreme achievement of the Sumerians. They were probably the first people in the world to develop a way of setting down their thoughts. At first, the Sumerians had used picture-writing. They had carved symbols on stone, or cut them into tablets of soft clay. As the centuries passed, the Sumerian picture-symbols evolved into something quite different: characters made up of many wedge-shaped marks, formed by pressing a sharp stylus into clay.

When barbarian invaders overthrew Sumer, they adapted cuneiform writing to their own Semitic languages. So the cuneiform-stamped bricks Layard found represented a kind of writing that had already been many thousands of years old when those bricks were inscribed. He dreamed of the day when the ancient writing could again be read— but would it ever be possible to do so, he wondered?

Layard bubbled with ambition. At Mosul, there were the mounds of Kouyunjik and Nebbi Yunus. A short way down the river, there was Nimroud. Further along, Qalah Shergat. And each one, he knew, concealed an ancient city! He resolved to explore them all, one day.

But not yet. They returned to Mosul and prepared for departure. The Tigris was now flooded by the melting of snow on the mountains to the north, and during the two-month period of high water the river could be navigated. *Keleks*, or rafts made of inflated sheepskins and goatskins fastened together by willow twigs, were the usual means of transportation. Reeds and planks were laid over the twigs, and a kind of hut of arched canes built atop them. One or two men would guide the rafts down the river, and when they reached their destination they would be broken up, the wood sold for fuel and the skins brought back on muleback for further use.

Mitford and Layard hired a *kelek*, after some nasty wrangling with its manufacturer, and on April 29, 1840, they left Mosul to float down to Baghdad. Their raft, twelve feet long and eight feet wide, had only one boatman.

They shot rapidly down the current in the middle of the river, and soon Mosul was lost to view. Late that afternoon, they drifted past the mound of Nimroud. Layard tells us that "The spring rains had clothed the mound with the richest verdure, and the fertile meadows, which stretched around it, were covered with flowers of every hue. Amidst this luxuriant vegetation were partly concealed a few fragments of bricks, pottery, and alabaster, upon which might be traced the well-defined wedges of the cuneiform character."

Soon after, they were carried over the remains of an ancient dam, probably Assyrian, and their boatman successfully got them through the foaming, dangerous rapids. From then on, it was a leisurely, relaxing journey, broken the next day by a stop to refill the skins of the raft, which had begun to leak air.

The succeeding day, after floating all night, they saw their first palm trees, and clusters of orange, citron and pomegranate trees in full bloom. "A gentle breeze wafted a delicious odor over the river, with the cooing of innumerable turtle-doves. The creaking of the water-wheels, worked by oxen, and the cries of the Arabs on the banks added life and animation to the scene. I thought that I had never seen anything so truly beautiful, and all my *Arabian Nights* dreams were almost more than realized."

The finest moment was yet ahead—at the following dawn, when the sun rose to reveal the gilded domes and minarets of Baghdad gleaming above the dense forest of palms through which the river now flowed. Layard and Mitford washed and changed into their best clothes, for the end of their raft journey was at hand. No sooner had Layard made himself tidy, though, than he slipped and fell headlong into the river. He was hauled forth, drenched to the skin, and he made his entry into Baghdad dripping wet.

"We continued to float through these endless groves of palmtrees," he writes, "the air laden with the delicious odor of the orange and citron trees, until, sweeping round a bend of the river, we came in sight of the city rising majestically on its banks—with its innumerable painted domes and minarets, its lofty walls and towers, its palaces and painted kiosks. It seemed to be all that I had pictured to myself of the city of the Caliphs and the sojourn of Haroun al-Rashid."

Alas for Scheherazade, the reality as viewed at close range did not match the vision at a distance. Entering Baghdad, Layard found that "Instead of the magnificent capital whose distant view had enchanted me, I was in the midst of an assemblage of mean, mud-built dwellings and a heap of ruins."

There was a large English colony at Baghdad, and after their wanderings in uncivilized realms Layard and Mitford welcomed the sound of polite conversation, the crisp accents of London-bred voices. Layard's time in Baghdad passed agreeably and too quickly. He was industrious, as usual—taking lessons in Persian, since Persia was his next destination. And, making friends with Colonel Taylor, who now served in Claudius Rich's old job of East India Company Resident at Baghdad, Layard used Taylor's vast library to learn all he could of the ancient history of the region, with particular emphasis on the Assyrians and Babylonians.

There were also mounds to visit, of course—the ruins of Babylon, at nearby Hillah. Babylon, once the capital of wise King Hammurabi, had fallen on evil days long ago. It had repeatedly been invaded by the Assyrians who lived to the north, and from about 1100 B.C. on, Babylon had been subject to Assyrian rule. Babylon often revolted against the Assyrians, and had met a ghastly fate at the decree of bloody-handed Sennacherib, who destroyed the city entirely when it dared to rise against him. Sennacherib left an inscription boasting of how he had burned Babylon, over-turned the smoldering ruins into the canal, and finally turned the river into the city to flood it completely.

Babylon had been rebuilt, though, during the reign of Sennacherib's son, Esarhaddon. The new city was far grander than the old, attaining dizzy heights of splendor under a later king, Nebuchadnezzar. But it tasted defeat again when the Persians invaded it, in 538 B.C., and in time it had come to disappear beneath desert sands. Claudius Rich, as we have seen, had visited the ruins of Babylon in 1811. Layard, familiar with Rich's books, went to have a look himself.

"I shall never forget," he wrote, "the effect produced upon me by the long lines and vast masses of mounds, which mark the site of ancient Babylon, as they appeared in the distance one morning as the day broke behind them. The desolation, the solitude, those shapeless heaps, all that remain of a great and renowned city, are well calculated to impress and excite the imagination."

He spent one whole day prowling the ruins under a blistering sun, accompanied only by a single Arab. Earlier, he had arranged to return to Baghdad on the steamer *Nitocris*, which traveled up and down the Tigris under a British captain. The steamer trip would spare him a hot, hard ride back over the plain.

Late in the day, busy at the ruins, Layard was surprised to see the smoke of the steamer in the distance. He hurried toward the river, only to find to his horror that a broad and deep marsh cut him off from the main stream.

He was alone and on foot, and an attack of fever was coming on. To return on foot to Baghdad was almost impossible. There was only one thing to do. Stripping off most of his clothing, Layard plunged into the swamp.

The water reached to his armpits, and he had to make his way through deep, clinging mud, with hot sunlight broiling his scalp. His rising fever made his progress even slower. He was afraid, too, that the commander of the steamer would think he was only an Arab buffalo-keeper, and would pass onward without stopping.

Layard frantically waved his handkerchief and shouted to the passing steamer. The commander, Layard tells us, "stopped his vessel and sent a boat to my assistance, in which I was taken to her. She was commanded by Captain Jones of the Indian Navy, whose acquaintance I thus made. He used in after years to speak of his surprise at seeing a man with his head above water, in a marsh far from all human habitation and in the desert, struggling and making the most desperate attempts to attract his notice, and at finding, when he sent to his rescue, that he was an English traveller."

IV

The time now had come for Layard and Mitford to make the great eastward trek that hopefully would bring them safely to Ceylon. The most difficult and dangerous part of their journey lay ahead: through Persia.

Layard dressed himself in Persian clothes. He had studied Persian diligently during his two months in Baghdad, but he did not, of course, expect to be able to pass himself off as a native. Nonetheless he thought the Persian outfit— long flowing robes bound at the waist by a shawl, loose trousers, and a tall black lambskin cap—would spare him from much difficulty. Not only was there political strain between Persia and England just then, but the Persians were fanatical Moslems, much more hostile to Europeans than were the Turks.

So by wearing Persian clothes he would at least not be calling attention to his alien nature. He went so far as to shave the crown of his head, leaving a ringlet on each side, and to dye his hair and beard a deep shining black after the Persian fashion. "I could thus pass very well," he says, "so long as my mouth was closed, for an orthodox Persian."

So wild was the country ahead that traveling alone seemed too risky for even the indomitable Layard and Mitford. They decided to join one of the caravans bound out of Baghdad for the interior of Persia. It was a procession of about seventy people riding horses, mules and donkeys, and led by two elderly Turkish guides. Since it was near the end of June, and close to the hottest part of the year, it was necessary to travel at night and rest by day to avoid the intense heat of the plains.

After an infuriating delay, the caravan finally departed from Baghdad on June 29, 1840, and soon crossed the border that separated Turkey from Persia. Layard and Mitford had left the land of the Sultan and entered the land of the Shah.

If Turkey had been in a state of confusion, Persia was then in absolute chaos. Its government was cruel and corrupt, even by easy-going Oriental standards. By Persian standards the Turks and Egyptians were models of efficiency, honesty and reliability. Only the western part of Persia obeyed the authority of the Shah at all; in the east, most of the local city governors had set themselves up as semi-independent little shahs, while the wild mountain tribesmen were in rebellion against all authority but their own.

The first few days of their Persian caravan-ride were uneventful. Near Kermanshah, the first Persian town they came to, Layard and Mitford paused to inspect the ancient sculptures at Tak-i-Bustan, only to find a pair of Europeans already on the spot and making sketches. They were two Frenchmen, an architect named Coste and an artist named Flandin. Layard would later encounter Flandin at Mosul, where he went to make sketches of Botta's Khorsabad finds, to be used as illustrations in a sumptuous book that the French government was planning to publish.

Soon Persia began to strike Layard as an unfriendly, even a sinister place. The fanatic Moslems glared at them constantly, cursed them as infidels, and had nothing otherwise to do with the two Englishmen. "They would not allow us to spread our carpets near the spot which they had chosen for their day's rest," Layard writes. "The women were made to pull down their veils whenever we approached them, and even the children were taught to run away from us as if we were infected with the plague."

The fact that they were Christians was compounded by the fact that England and Persia were at the brink of war. Some of their traveling companions in the caravan were convinced that Layard and Mitford were spies for England.

There was soon the usual difficulty about a *firman*, or permit from the Shah allowing them to travel in Persia. At Kermanshah they were informed by the local governor that they could go no farther until such a *firman* had been obtained. Luckily, the Shah was then encamped only a three days' journey away.

Getting to see the Shah proved a taxing challenge, for no sooner did Layard and Mitford set out to see him than word came that the monarch had broken camp and was moving elsewhere. After some haggling, the travelers received permission to leave Kermanshah and follow along.

On the way, naturally, they found time to inspect more ancient monuments—this time the celebrated rock sculptures at Bisutun, or Behistun. Here, hundreds of feet above the ground, artists had cut into the face of a cliff a pictorial relief, and a cuneiform inscription in three columns. No one could then translate cuneiform, and so the nature of the inscription was unknown. But, as we will see, the Behistun Rock inscription was to provide an important link in the chain of events that led to the rediscovery of lost Assyria.

Layard was no more able to read the inscription than anyone else. He could not even copy it, since it was at such an inaccessible height. He simply stared, and marveled, and moved on.

They traveled fifteen miles through marshes after leaving Behistun, their horses continually sinking in, and the croaking of innumerable frogs deafening everyone. Finally they came to the village of Sanna, where they halted.

"It was July 8," writes Layard. "Just one year since I had left England on my adventurous journey. I was still in high spirits, deeply interested in all that I was seeing, enjoying to the full my independent mode of life, ready to face any further perils and difficulties, and in excellent health, notwithstanding the attacks of intermittent fever from which I had occasionally suffered, but which did not appear to have produced any permanent effect upon my naturally robust constitution."

They came to the Shah's encampment, and applied for their *firman*. The Shah had thought perhaps of invading Baghdad—Persia was on bad terms with her neighbor Turkey as well as with England—but, giving up the idea, was slowly returning to his court at Teheran. Layard found him at Hamadan, with his entire court and a shabby, menacing-looking army.

A month of maddening delay ensued before Layard and Mitford received the all-important *firman*. The officials of the court were uneasy about the two Englishmen, who might, after all, be spies. Furthermore, most of eastern Persia was in revolt against the Shah, and the Shah's ministers were unwilling to let the wanderers enter such dangerous territory for fear of provoking some new trouble with England should they be murdered.

They saw the Prime Minister of Persia. "I will grant you the *firman*," he told them. "But first you must sign a declaration stating that you chose your route against my advice, and that I am not responsible for your safety."

Layard was willing to sign. Mitford, though, drew him aside and pointed out an important fact:

"Suppose they think we're spies? Once we've signed this paper of theirs, they're free to have us slaughtered out in the mountains. England won't be able to protest—not after we signed a statement releasing Persia from all responsibility for what happens to us!"

The discussion went on and on. The coming of August saw them still mired in Hamadan, applying for the *firman*. During the delay, Layard conceived an entirely new scheme for his travels.

He would give up the idea of going eastward toward the Indian frontier. Instead, he would go to Isfahan and then travel southward through the wild country of the Bakhtiyari tribesmen. This would avoid the dangerous country the Prime Minister warned against, and would also allow him to visit the ruins of the ancient city of Susa.

Mitford, though, still had every intention of reaching Ceylon that year, and he was less interested in old cities than his companion. He decided to take a northerly route, through a not very interesting but relatively safe part of Persia, to Afghanistan and thence to India.

There was no way of resolving the disagreement. The two friends agreed to separate. On August 8, the *firmans* finally came through, and they parted, Mitford for the north, Layard for Isfahan and the south. The *firman* Layard held was a generous one, as if to make up for its long delay in arriving. He was to travel at the Shah's expense. He would be furnished, without payment, with horses, and at each town where he stopped the inhabitants were required to supply him with provisions for eight persons, including chicken, meat, eggs, rice, bread, sugar, and much else. The Shah appointed a *mehmandar*, or official guide, to accompany Layard, protect him, and see that the *firman* was obeyed. He also provided him with a letter of

44

introduction to the governor of Isfahan, and one to Me
hemet Taki Khan, an important chief of the wild, rebellious Bakhtiyari tribesmen.

On August 9, Layard and his *mehmandar*, a Persian
named Imaum Verdi Beg, set out for Isfahan.

Layard speedily discovered that the *mehmandar* was
no paragon of virtue. At each village where they stopped,
the official insisted on extorting from the townsfolk the full
quality of provisions provided for by the *firman*. Since this
was far more than the two of them needed, Imaum Verdi
Beg would load the surplus on a donkey and carry it along,
selling it for his own private profit. Layard's liberal conscience rebelled at the idea of exploiting the poverty-
stricken people among whom he traveled, and he hated
Imaum Verdi's bullying attitude toward the peasants.

But there was no getting rid of the *mehmandar*. Layard tried to dismiss him, but the Persian refused to go. "I
am responsible for your welfare," Imaum Verdi told him
piously.

They reached Isfahan—"the city of the nightingales"
—and Layard was happy to part there with his Persian
companion. In that city, he met the governor of Isfahan, a
cruel, sinister eunuch known as the Matamet, who received Layard courteously enough, and agreed to help him
continue his journey. The Matamet passed Layard along to
a Bakhtiyari chieftain called Shefi'a Khan, who happened
to be in Isfahan at that time. Shefi'a Khan was willing to
conduct the Englishman into the wild Bakhtiyari country.

There were the customary delays, and weeks went by.
Layard's stay in Isfahan was rendered more pleasant by the
presence there of a number of Europeans. He visited
among them, meeting once again Flandin and Coste, who
had come here to sketch more ruins.

On September 22, Shefi'a Khan told Layard that he was ready to leave, and they set out on their journey into the Bakhtiyari lands. Layard's sojourn there was a lengthy one, and his many adventures among the wild tribesmen fill hundreds of pages of his own autobiographical narratives. He spent months among them, much of his time with the Bakhtiyari chieftain Mehemet Taki Khan and his family.

Mehemet Taki Khan was an unusual Persian, it seems —noble, honest, dignified. He befriended Layard and treated him well, and the pages in which Layard tells of his life among the Bakhtiyari are some of the happiest in his books.

Layard practically became a member of Mehemet Taki Khan's family. He first won Mehemet Taki Khan's affection by curing his best-beloved son of fever. The boy was seriously ill, and his mother implored Layard to save him. Having had plenty of experience with fever himself, Layard gave her some doses of quinine to administer to the lad.

But two local physicians were already handling the case. They preferred traditional remedies, such as bathing the boy in melon-juice and wine, and having him drink water with which the inside of a porcelain coffee-cup, on which a text from the Koran was written in ink, had been washed. Naturally they forbade the use of any infidel medicines Layard had to offer.

The boy worsened and neared death. Again his mother came to Layard in tears.

"Did you give him the medicines I prescribed?" Layard asked.

"No. The other doctors would not allow it. And now he is dying!"

Mehemet Taki Khan himself begged Layard to heal his son. Layard pointed out that the two Moslem physicians had thwarted him once. He refused to act unless they were kept from interfering. Reluctantly, the two doctors withdrew from the case. Layard now dipped into his medicine kit and administered a dose of something known as "Dover's powder," a fever remedy. Then he spent an anxious night. If the boy recovered, Mehemet Taki Kahn would be forever indebted to him—but if he died, Layard knew he might be blamed for his death, and even accused by the native doctors of having poisoned the child.

About midnight, the boy broke into a violent perspiration, and his fever broke. The next day he was better, and soon was on the way to complete recovery. Layard had won his way into the hearts of the Bakhtiyari, and from then on they refused him nothing.

Until a feud began between Mehemet Taki Khan and the Matamet, Layard was able to tour the Bakhtiyari country at will and without fear of danger, exploring the ruins of Susa and the outlying districts. Susa had once been the capital of an ancient people called the Elamites, more than four thousand years ago, and later, after the downfall of Assyria and Babylonia, had been an important city in the great Persian Empire of 500 to 350 B.C.

It puzzled Mehemet Taki Khan that Layard should have come so far, and faced such great dangers and hardships, merely to look at some dead cities. "He could scarcely believe," Layard writes, "that I had been impelled to do so by the love of adventure, and by a curiosity to visit new countries and to explore ancient remains." Rather, he suspected, Layard was a secret agent of the British Government, collecting information useful to the invasion of Persia by England. "But he so hated the corrupt, vicious, and cruel Persians, and was so exasperated at the constant demands upon him for money by the Persian governor of Isfahan, that he was not the less friendly to me on that account," wrote Layard.

Layard spent most of that autumn searching for ruins in Bakhtiyari country. If he had ever seriously thought of getting to Ceylon promptly, he abandoned the idea now, and gave his curiosity full rein.

The natives, knowing he was interested in antiquities, went out of their way to invent some for him. Time and again he made a difficult and risky expedition to view some supposed inscription or monument that had been described for him, only to find nothing but "a few heaps of stone, or the ruined walls of a building of a comparatively recent period, and some natural marks on a weather-beaten cliff, in which a lively imagination had detected the writing of the Franks."

As he ventured farther and farther from the area Mehemet Taki Khan controlled, he came under suspicion. At a place that was supposedly the tomb of the prophet Daniel, he was given a searching cross-examination by a local chieftain. He was the first European ever seen in those parts. "Was I a Christian, and consequently unclean? They had heard of Georgians and Armenians, was I either the one or the other? What was the object of my journey? Had I seen in my books that a treasure was concealed at Sûsan, and did I know and could I point out to them the place where it was buried? Were the Feringhi [Europeans] about to take possession of the country? and innumerable questions of that kind."

They appeared to decide that he was either a magician, to whom the djinns had given the power of finding buried gold, or a secret agent sent to spy out the land. Layard blandly told them that he was a pilgrim, who had come from afar to view the tomb of Daniel, and this seemed to soothe them.

At the tomb itself, though, a half-crazy dervish spied him and hauled out a gun. "He is a Feringhi! He is unclean!" the fanatic cried. He threatened to shoot Layard unless he repeated at once the Moslem profession of faith, "There is no god but God, and Mohammed is His Prophet."

For Layard, who had fought to keep Catholic boys from rubbing his nose against a chalked cross fifteen years before, making such a declaration was all but impossible— even at the risk of his life. Luckily, the dervish was disarmed, and Layard left the holy spot before further troubles could ensue.

With winter drawing near, Layard returned to the castle of Mehemet Taki Khan soon afterward. It was a season of storms, with thunder, lightning and high winds. During one such storm a pack of wolves descended on the Bakhtiyari camp, breaking through the tents and carrying off nine sheep.

Layard now became drawn into the feud between Mehemet Taki Khan and the Matamet. Though, as a tourist, Layard was supposed to keep out of local conflicts, he was so impressed with the Bakhtiyari chieftain that he went so far as to become a messenger for Mehemet Taki Khan, intriguing on his behalf, and even took part in an armed attack on the Matamet's troops in an attempt to rescue his friend from captivity. These operations kept Layard busy through the first half of 1841. Two years had passed since his departure from England, and he was still far from Ceylon.

He shortly learned that the entire district ahead of him,

both in eastern Persia and along the borders of India, was in revolt and confusion. To venture further toward the east at this time would be foolhardy. Layard decided, therefore, to go back to Baghdad and wait there until matters were less fluid in the east.

V

As long as he had to return, Layard saw no reason to cover ground he had once traveled. He picked out a southern route back to Baghdad via the Persian Gulf seaport of Basra.

Getting there entangled him in the robberies and hardships to which he was by now thoroughly accustomed. Entering Basra at sunset, he spied a ship flying the English flag, and began to board it. The sailor on guard at the gangway, seeing what appeared to be a poor Arab clad in tatters, warned him off, and was immensely startled to be answered in English!

A few days in Basra and Layard was ready to begin the next leg of his return to Baghdad. An Arab postman employed by the Indian Government was about to leave Basra with mail bound for Baghdad, and Layard wangled permission to accompany him. He was warned of the dangers of the journey. Postmen were often robbed and even maltreated by the wild tribes through which they had to pass. Layard would have to ride day and night without much rest, and he would find little water in the desert that lay ahead.

"As I was by this time inured to heat and hardships," he notes, "I trusted to my usual good fortune to get through the threatened difficulties and dangers."

The trip was an eventful one, marked by narrow escapes from marauders, great privation, and constant danger. He was robbed no less than three times between Basra and Baghdad. The first time he benefited from his usual good luck in escaping serious harm. But the second robbery was nearly a disaster. He was set upon by a party of Shammar Arabs, murderous marauders who were particularly incensed against the Turks. The Shammars galloped up, their spears at the ready, and Layard and the postman were thrown from their horses. Layard's cloak fell away, revealing a red Turkish *fez* that he had donned to protect his head from the sun.

"*Toork!*" the Arabs cried. "*Toork!*"

A moment later there was a knife at Layard's chest. Desperately he called out that he was no Turk but an Englishman. One of the Arabs mistook him for Dr. Ross, an English doctor residing at Baghdad, and said, "Leave him alone. He tells the truth. He is my friend, and the English are the friends of our tribe."

Layard's life was spared—but not his property. The other Shammar, losing no time, had plundered Layard's saddle-bags, and refused to restore what they had already taken. They made off with his horse, his watch, his compass, his few remaining silver pieces—and his gown, shoes, and stockings as well. Layard was left with nothing but his *fez*, his Arab shirt, and his *abba*, a goat-hair cloak.

He was still some hours distant from Baghdad. Grateful enough that his life had been spared, Layard began the barefoot journey. The ground, heated by the sun, burned the soles of his feet, and soon he was blistered and bleeding.

Layard and the postman hurried on. Night fell, but they continued to force themselves toward Baghdad, since if they were caught in the desert by the rising sun they would surely perish of heat and thirst. Their adventures were not yet over, however. Two Arabs on foot appeared, armed with short, heavy clubs. They demanded Layard's clothes. Wearily, he turned over to them his *fez* and his *abba*, receiving in exchange the ragged cloak of one of the thieves. A single threadbare garment hid Layard's nakedness now. Without the protection of his *fez*, he knew he had to hurry on to Baghdad, for his shaven scalp would suffer under the rays of the desert sun.

As dawn broke, Baghdad appeared, and a boatman was found who would take the tired travelers across the Tigris to the city. They drew near a gate—but it would not be opened until sunrise. Layard sank down, overcome with fatigue and pain, and waited.

At length the gate was thrown open. Two servants of the English Residency emerged, splendid in their gold-embroidered uniforms. They carried whips with which they drove aside the Arabs clustered outside the gate, to make way for a party of mounted European ladies and gentlemen. They were Layard's old Baghdad friends, out for a morning ride.

He writes, "They passed close to me, but did not recognize me in the dirty Arab in rags crouched near the entrance, nor, clothed as I was, could I venture to make myself known to them. But at a little distance behind them came Dr. Ross. I called to him, and he turned towards me in the utmost surprise, scarcely believing his senses when he saw me without cover to my bare head, with naked feet, and in my tattered *abba*."

And so, blistered and bare of foot and nearly naked, Austen Henry Layard entered Baghdad for the second time.

After a few days in bed, the amazing Layard felt cheerful and full of energy again, though it was a long while before he could walk without pain or discomfort.

His first task in Baghdad was to answer some of the mail that had piled up there for him during his long absence in Persia. His family had not heard from him in months, and perhaps thought he was dead.

On September 8, 1841, Layard wrote to his uncle, Benjamin Austen, recounting some of his hair-raising adventures:

"Thank God I am again among Europeans and countrymen," Layard told his uncle. "Long absence had rendered me a complete Persian."

Still undecided about whether to go to Ceylon at all, Layard took up residence in Baghdad, renting a small mud hut not far from the mansion of the East India Company Resident, Colonel Taylor. During the day, Layard browsed in Taylor's library, studied different languages, and worked on a narrative of his travels thus far. By night, he slept on the roof of his hut, under the stars, to cope with the heat.

Two months passed this way. By November, the restless Layard was eager to return to Persia, complete his researches among the ruins of Susa, and find out what had become of his friend Mehemet Taki Khan. A glutton for punishment, Layard roamed the Bakhtiyari country all over again, finding little in the way of archaeological importance and frequently jeopardizing his life. The news about Mehemet Taki Khan was grim. The Bakhtiyari chief had been treacherously tricked by the Matamet, and was a miserable prisoner now, his property confiscated and many of his close relatives murdered. He was destined never to be released from captivity.

Layard returned to Baghdad early in 1842. Letters were waiting for him from home. There had been a change for the worse in his family's financial position, and his mother wondered if he might perhaps be willing to return to England.

The idea of going to Ceylon, which had seemed so appealing in 1839, now struck Layard as impractical and unreal. He abandoned it completely, and decided to go home. Before leaving, though, he felt he had to carry out one more investigation—a trip up the Karun River, to find out whether or not it was suited for navigation. This, he felt, would take him a month.

The little steamer *Assyria*, in which he made the journey, unfortunately ran aground on a shoal, and it took a month simply to refloat the vessel. So Layard did not return to Baghdad until May 1842—having proved, though, that the Karun was navigable with proper caution.

At long last Layard prepared to go home, crossing the Mesopotamian desert to Damascus, then to Beirut, where he would take ship to England. Suddenly word came from Constantinople that Turkey was about to declare war on Persia. There had been a quarrel over the Turkish-Persian border, the Persians had seized possession of an important port belonging to Turkey, and the Sultan was ready to fight for Turkey's rights.

Britain and Persia had recently quarreled also. And Britain was then on friendly terms with Turkey. So it looked as if Britain might get involved in a Turkish-Persian war, fighting on Turkey's side. It was of the highest importance that Sir Stratford Canning, the British Ambassador to Turkey, get all possible information on the dispute at once, so London could work out strategy.

Now it happened that Layard had just returned from the precise region where the Turks and Persians had come to blows. Nobody knew the situation more intimately than the adventurous English traveler. Obviously he was the man to give Sir Stratford the necessary briefing. Colonel Taylor, the English Resident in Baghdad, sought Layard out.

"Change your itinerary," Taylor told him. "Go home by way of Constantinople and see Sir Stratford. Give him a first-hand report on everything you've seen in Persia."

Layard was delighted. At 25, after three years of the most grueling sort of travel, he had come to think of himself—with some justice—as an expert on the Orient and on Orientals. Now the world of English officialdom said it needed his special knowledge!

He set out at once. Because of the urgency of the situation, he rode day and night to Mosul, where dispatches were being prepared that Layard was to carry to Sir Stratford. It took fifty hours of harrowing riding through the June heat of the Assyrian plains to cover the 250 miles from Baghdad to Mosul.

There was a three-day delay in Mosul while the dispatches were prepared. Layard, who liked to mix archaeology with his adventure, put aside his role as secret agent for the moment. He took advantage of the delay to inspect the Assyrian mounds, which he had first seen more than two years before.

And now Layard had a chance to meet one of the key figures in Mesopotamian archaeology—Paul Emile Botta, who, like Layard, had read the books of Claudius Rich and had become enthusiastic about the ruined cities of Mesopotamia.

Botta, a diplomat in the French foreign service, was the son of a famous Italian historian. His chief interests were in the field of botany, but he was a cultivated and scientific man who took all knowledge for his province. He had been employed for a while in the French consular service in China, and there had developed the habit of smoking opium. It had ruined his health, and left him troubled with fits of melancholy and despair.

Still smoking the deadly narcotic, Botta received a transfer to Mosul, and by late 1840 he found himself French Consul there. And across the river were the great mounds of which Rich had written! Botta was determined to explore them.

He began at the mound called Kouyunjik. Some excavation there turned up very little: some scraps of brick and alabaster, a few cuneiform characters, nothing more. Discouraged by the difficulty of the work, Botta had abandoned the project. When Layard reached Mosul in 1842, Botta had halted work. Hearing that the new French Consul had done some actual excavating, Layard sought the diplomat out.

The two men took to one another immediately. Together they crossed the river to inspect the mounds of Kouyunjik and Nebbi Yunus. Layard was sure that the fragments found by Botta indicated some great ruin deeper in the mound. Although Layard was desperately eager to dig in Kouyunjik himself, he knew it would be impossible for him to do so at that time, and perhaps he might never have the opportunity. He urged Botta to try again. The Consul, though, was unenthusiastic. He was, he told Layard, looking hopefully for some more fruitful mound to explore.

They parted on good terms—though not before Botta had persuaded Layard to sample the delights of opium, to which he himself was already addicted. Layard smoked an opium pipe. "The result, happily, was that I suffered from so severe a headache, accompanied by violent sickness, that I have never made a second attempt, and have held the very smell of opium in abhorrence ever since." Botta urged Layard to persevere and cultivate a taste for the narcotic, but the Englishman wisely refused.

The dispatches were now ready, and Layard departed for Constantinople—once again riding helter-skelter, day and night. He arrived in the Turkish capital on July 9, bronzed and unkempt after his long journey, and dressed in a ragbag mixture of Eastern and European clothes.

He hastened to the British Embassy to deliver his dispatches. A servant confronted him. "I bear messages for Sir Stratford Canning," Layard announced.

"You will please wait."

Layard waited. He waited quite a long while indeed, and his patience was running thin when "at length a fashionably-dressed young gentleman appeared, asked me cavalierly for the dispatches of which I was the bearer, informed me that the Ambassador was too much occupied to see any one, and turning on his heel left the room without deigning to listen to what I had to say."

Layard was furious. He demanded of the other Embassy officials that he be taken to see Sir Stratford at once. But the fastidious, well-groomed young men of the Embassy were appalled by this wild-looking stranger. Layard was none too politely shown the door.

Unable to speak to Sir Stratford, he had no choice but to leave Constantinople and continue his journey toward England. Before departing, though, he dashed off a hot-headed, ill-tempered letter to the Ambassador, protesting at the treatment he had received. Having traveled night and day from Baghdad, he felt he was entitled at the very least to a personal interview with Sir Stratford.

Layard was mainly interested in blowing off steam at that point. He did not expect a reply. He was astonished, then, when a messenger from the British Embassy arrived a few hours later, inviting Layard to call on the Ambassador at once.

The following morning Layard was shown into the Ambassador's presence. Sir Stratford struck him as one of the handsomest men he had ever seen—tall and white-haired, somewhat stoop-shouldered, with earnest gray eyes and a look of vast dignity. In Layard's words, "His thin, compressed lips denoted a violent and passionate temper. His complexion was so transparent that the least emotion —whether of pleasure or of anger—was shown at once by its varying tints. A broad, massive and overhanging brow gave him an air of profound wisdom and sagacity. He was altogether a very formidable-looking personage."

But his manner was kindly and considerate. He apologized for the rude manners of the young men of the Embassy, who had, he assured Layard, been reprimanded. He proceeded to question Layard about the events on the Turkish-Persian border, and after a long conversation said, "Your knowledge of the territory can be of great use to me. England hopes to avoid this war by mediating between the Sultan and the Shah."

Sir Stratford asked Layard to remain in Constantinople for a short while, in case further information was needed from him. Layard agreed, and postponed his sailing.

Several weeks passed. Nothing was heard from Sir Stratford. Layard's funds were running low, and he had barely enough money to see him home to England. He wrote to Canning, telling him that unless there was need of his services, he would return to England in a few days. There was no reply, and Layard assumed that Canning had lost interest in him. He booked passage on a ship bound for Vienna, and, packing his few belongings, began to descend the steep street to the wharf where he was to embark.

Only minutes before he was about to board the ship, Layard was approached by a messenger from the British Embassy, who had followed him from his hotel to the dock. He bore a note from Sir Stratford Canning, telling Layard that he had an assignment for him. "Instead of going away," the Ambassador wrote, "Come and dine here tomorrow, and I will try to arrange a plan with you."

Layard cancelled his departure. England would have to get along without him for a while longer—though he probably did not realize then that it would be another five years before he actually got home.

VI

The next day, Layard saw the Ambassador. Sir Stratford told him that England and Russia had intervened in the quarrel between Turkey and Persia. Mediation was under way, but the negotiations were moving slowly, and it would be some time before Sir Stratford would need the special information Layard could supply.

In the meanwhile, Canning had a different assignment. The Turkish provinces in Europe were in a state of crisis and unrest. Would Layard care to visit Bosnia and Serbia, then under Turkish rule (now parts of Yugoslavia) and report on conditions there?

"You will not, of course, have any official character or mission," the Ambassador told him. "You will simply be a traveler in those lands. But what you see, you will report to me."

Layard liked the idea of becoming a British secret agent, and accepted the assignment. On August 20, 1842, he left Constaninople bound for Turkey-in-Europe. He was in high spirits, for at last he saw a possibility for permanent employment. If he discharged his secret mission to Sir Stratford's satisfaction, he might receive an official diplomatic appointment in the East. This would allow him to carry on private archaeological explorations, after the fashion of that other diplomat, Botta.

He roamed through Serbia, Bosnia and Albania, making careful observations on the various insurrections in progress in those troubled lands. Some months later he returned to Constantinople and delivered a full and highly satisfactory report to Sir Stratford. Several important British foreign policy decisions were based directly on the information Layard brought back.

Sir Stratford was delighted with Layard's work. Unfortunately, word trickled back to London, to Lord Aberdeen, the British Foreign Minister and Sir Stratford's superior, that the new British policy—which Lord Aberdeen disliked—was largely the work of a young wanderer named Layard.

Layard found himself caught in a policy dispute between Sir Stratford and Lord Aberdeen. Aberdeen developed a lively prejudice against Layard, and blocked any chance of an official post for him. This was, of course, a grave disappointment.

Although he had not succeeded in getting on the British diplomatic payroll, Layard was still needed in Constantinople. The mediation in the Turkish-Persian quarrel was at a critical stage, and Layard knew more about the border area in question than anyone else. "Stay in Constantinople," Canning told him. "I'll request an appointment for you from Lord Aberdeen."

Layard stayed. As a confidential assistant to the Ambassador, he soon found himself in a position of trust, and Sir Stratford willingly accepted the advice of his young unofficial attaché. Sir Stratford was in touch with certain Turkish political leaders who were attempting to lead a reform movement in Turkey, and Layard became the Ambassador's go-between.

Now Layard became a secret agent in earnest. He could speak a little Turkish, and he had had plenty of experience with the Turkish psychology. So he was sent on delicate, difficult and dangerous missions, visiting the leaders of the Turkish reform movement. Some of them held high Turkish office, but others were in disgrace and forced retirement. It would have been highly suspicious for an Englishman to be seen visiting them. Layard had to make his diplomatic rounds under cover of darkness, always with the greatest secrecy. The Turks soon became fond of the handsome, fearless young Englishman, so different from the fussy, haughty bureaucrats they had known before.

We can be certain that Layard enjoyed his role to the hilt. How he must have delighted in skulking about Constantinople on moonless nights, slipping into Oriental palaces through side entrances to hold whispered conversations with important Turkish leaders!

He also busied himself preparing a report on the Turkish-Persian border dispute. He examined all the evidence—a mass of documents, maps and surveys, many of them of ancient date—and worked out a draft of a proposed settlement. Having seen the area himself, he felt that there was no doubt but that the land in question belonged to Turkey, and he told Sir Stratford as much. Canning agreed, and Layard's document was approved and adopted as the official British position.

Unhappily, Russia, the fourth party in the negotiations, had backed Persia's claim. Lord Aberdeen, the chief British negotiator, had reasons of his own for not wanting to offend Russia just then, and bowed to Russian demands. The mediation was decided in favor of Persia, and Layard's proposal was discarded. When word reached Constantinople of this, Canning sent for Layard.

Layard found him "walking up and down his study, his brows knit, his thin lips compressed, and his delicate complexion scarlet with anger. Without saying a word he handed me the dispatch. I read it, and remarked that I was deeply grieved to find that Lord Aberdeen had come to a decision which, in my opinion, was not consistent with justice and right, and was not in the interests of England."

Canning and Layard drew up a new document, a letter of protest to Lord Aberdeen. But Aberdeen would not be moved, and the decision in favor of Persia stood. Annoyed by Layard's opposition, Aberdeen also turned down Canning's request that Layard be given an appointment to the Embassy staff, or that he be named one of the two commissioners who would decide the new Turkish-Persian boundary.

For the next two years, Layard remained at Constantinople, serving Sir Stratford in high matters of state, and waiting with dwindling hopes for some kind of official post. Money was becoming a serious problem for him. Sir Stratford was in no position to contribute much to his upkeep by way of private salary. Layard's funds were all but exhausted.

He was desperate. So desperate, in fact, that he took the drastic step of writing Benjamin Austen in England, to ask his uncle if there might now be room for him in the law firm. Before an answer came, Layard received a reprieve. A friend of his, Colonel White, had been writing a series of articles on Constantinople for a London newspaper, the *Morning Post*. The Colonel was now returning to England. Did Layard care to take over the job?

Layard did. He became Turkish correspondent for the *Post* at a salary of £150—$750—a year. In addition, he was hired to write other articles for the *Malta Times*, at a small extra sum. It was not a magnificent income, but it was enough to keep him alive if he lived economically. He found a place to live where room and board together cost him only $20 a month, and began his new career as a newspaper correspondent.

One of the first items of news he sent back to Europe was a startling one: the French Consul at Mosul, M. Botta, had dug in a mound near the city, and had unearthed astonishing treasures. Botta had found nothing less than an Assyrian palace!

Botta had been busy since Layard last saw him. Despite Layard's urgings, the French diplomat had not done any more digging at Kouyunjik. Nor had he investigated the mound of Nimroud, which Layard had also suggested to him as a possible excavation site.

Instead, word had come to Botta of another mound fourteen miles north of Mosul, called Khorsabad. There were reports that "sculptured stones" had been found there.

Suspicious of native rumors, Botta sent a consular agent to have a look. The man hired a couple of workmen and drove a well in the mound. A short distance from the surface, they came upon a buried wall built of slabs of gypsum.

Botta hurried to the site in March 1843, and himself supervised the digging of a wide trench. Almost at once, wonderful things came to light: limestone slabs covered with elaborate and artistic scenes. The vivid reliefs showed stern-visaged bearded men, sieges, battles of the most savage kind, weird and grotesque animals. And everywhere along the slabs were lengthy cuneiform inscriptions.

He sent word immediately to Paris: "I believe myself to be the first who has discovered sculptures which with some reason can be referred to the period when Nineveh was flourishing."

He was right. To Paul Emile Botta goes the credit for

having been the first to excavate an Assyrian city. But which city? No one knew, since no one could yet read the copious cuneiform inscriptions that covered every slab Botta found. The clue existed, but no one immediately seized it. Certain Arab geographical texts declared that Khorsabad occupied the site of an Assyrian city called "Saraoun" or "Saraghoun." These statements were ignored.

A decade went by before the old Arab traditions could be confirmed by translation of the Khorsabad texts. The city Botta had found was Dur-Sharrukin, built by the Assyrian King Sargon II about 710 B.C.

Botta laid bare more than a hundred chambers, halls and corridors. Then a dismaying thing began to happen: the limestone slabs, buried so long, began to fall to pieces on exposure to the air. The exquisite bas-reliefs were crumbling. "No precaution could arrest this rapid decay," Layard wrote, "and it was to be feared that this wonderful monument had only been uncovered to complete its ruin. The records of victories and triumphs, which had long attested the power and swelled the pride of the Assyrian kings, and had resisted the ravages of ages, were now passing away for ever."

The preservation of the slabs was further hampered by the behavior of the natives of Khorsabad. Botta inserted wooden struts to keep the uncovered slabs from falling, but at night the natives stole into the excavation and made off with the useful wood, letting the fragile slabs topple and break. The colossal stone statue of a bull was unearthed, and Botta attempted to bring it to Mosul, but had to abandon it midway when the sledge it was being drawn on collapsed. The peasants, taking it for an evil idol, destroyed it.

The French government, luckily, was aware of the historical and artistic value of Botta's sensational find. When

Botta's reports reached Paris, it was immediately decided to appropriate a large sum to reimburse Botta for his expenses in conducting the excavation. Furthermore, since the reliefs and sculptures were in immediate danger of destruction, an experienced artist was sent out from Paris to make careful and detailed drawings of everything that was found, so at least some record would be made before the Assyrian wonders crumbled to powder.

The artist chosen was Flandin, Layard's old friend from Persian days. He did not reach Khorsabad until May 1844, by which time much had been lost. Flandin immediately set to work, and his drawings were ultimately published at great expense by the French government in a large and costly book.

Botta's dispatches to Paris, and Flandin's drawings, had to pass through Constantinople on their way to Europe. Botta and Layard were in constant correspondence over the discoveries, and Botta arranged with the French post office in Constantinople that Layard would be allowed to examine the drawings and descriptions as they passed through the city.

How Layard's eyes must have gleamed as he leafed through Flandin's exciting sketches, as he read Botta's glowing accounts of his finds! With Botta's permission, Layard wrote about them for the *Malta Times*, and so it fell to Layard to give the world the first public account of the Assyrian discoveries.

Layard was too open-hearted a man to have felt any sense of disappointment at the fact that Botta, and not he, had made the first finds. Nor did he feel envious. He was delighted that *someone* had finally made the attempt—and, if it could not have been himself, it was just as well that it had been his friend Botta.

All the same, Layard itched with impatience to try his own hand at archaeology. There were plenty of other mounds around Mosul. Despite Botta's failure there, Layard was still convinced that Kouyunjik held promise. And there was Nimroud, eighteen miles down the river from Mosul, which also almost certainly held an Assyrian city.

He began to prepare for his own attempt. Because he thought (rightly, as it turned out) that the Assyrians had spoken a Semitic language, he devoted hours each day to the study of Hebrew, Syriac and other Semitic languages, in the hope that he might be able to break the code of cuneiform and translate the Assyrian inscriptions. He pored over works on Persian, Assyrian, and Babylonian history.

Layard still had a lingering hope that an official appointment would be given him. Without funds, he could hardly hope to excavate. Sir Stratford was still working on his behalf, but without luck. "He did the best he could to reconcile me to the disappointment," Layard wrote, "preaching patience and confidence—virtues which, under the circumstances, it was very needful to possess. To give me a proof of his desire to serve me he offered to present me to the Sultan."

The supreme ruler of Turkey, Sultan Abdul-Mejid, did not impress Layard, who found him "kind-hearted and well-intentioned . . . but constitutionally weak and feeble. . . . Small in stature and pale. . . ."

Before any archaeology, there was more diplomatic work for Layard. A revolt had arisen in Albania, and word was that the Albanian rebels had treated the Christian residents of that province of Turkey with shocking cruelty. Sir Stratford Canning regarded the welfare of all Christians in the Near East as his own responsibility. On May 1,

1844, he sent Layard to Albania to report on the true state of affairs there.

Layard visited the rebels, who were indeed oppressing the Christians, and tried to negotiate peace between the insurgents and the Turkish authorities. The rebels agreed to cease molesting Christians, but otherwise the rebellion continued, until the Turks broke it by capturing the Albanian leaders after promising them safe conduct. His mission not overly successful, Layard returned to Constantinople.

He arrived in July. Sir Stratford invited him to take up residence with him. He was given a small house in a garden adjoining the Ambassador's residence. Since Layard was to all intents and purposes a member of the Embassy staff, Sir Stratford gave him a small salary out of the general fund, though Layard held no official appointment.

In the summer of 1845, Sir Stratford made arrangements to return to England for a brief leave. He promised to speak personally with Lord Aberdeen, and to secure the diplomatic appointment for which Layard had been waiting so long.

In the meanwhile, there was the question of what Layard would do during Sir Stratford's absence. His funds were lower than ever, and there was no pressing diplomatic work that required his services.

He had never given up hope of exploring the ruins of Nineveh. Botta's spectacular successes at Khorsabad whetted Layard's eagerness. He approached Sir Stratford with a proposition: he would spend the fall and winter at Mosul, excavating at Kouyunjik and Nimroud, if only the Ambassador would give him financial assistance.

Canning agreed. Layard's own funds came to £60, or $300. Sir Stratford matched that with £60 of his own.

That would be enough to enable Layard to begin work. Both he and the Ambassador were sure that if Layard's digging bore results, the British government would contribute many thousands of pounds to underwrite the cost of excavating Nineveh. After all, had not France voted huge sums to finance Botta's work? Could Great Britain afford to do less?

It was decided. In October 1845, with the worst of the hot weather over, Layard departed from Constantinople. Destination: Nineveh!

VII

The adventure on which Layard was now embarking was quite different from his earlier exploits in the Near East. For one thing, he had a specific archaeological purpose in mind. For another, he now traveled in a semi-official capacity, with the blessing of the British Ambassador to Turkey and of the Sultan himself.

His preparations for this new trip were careful. He took lessons in surveying and mapping, learning how to make astronomical observations. There was no longer any need for him to take language instructions, since after six years in the East he spoke both Turkish and Arabic perfectly. He traveled light, taking with him some linens, a change or two of clothes, his books, and a few maps and instruments.

Nine hundred miles separates Constantinople and Mosul. Today, it is a plane trip of about two hours. Layard needed twelve days to make the journey—riding night and day, as was his habit, and passing through driving rainstorms most of the way. He reached Mosul on October 27, 1845, and took up residence with the British Vice-Consul, Christian Rassam, for the time being.

Mosul was then a town of about 40,000. Today it boasts its own airport and railway station, a first-class hotel, and clean, well kept streets. In Layard's day, though, it was a grim, foreboding place, which one traveler described this way:

"By night robbers stalk untouched from house to

house, and the time of rest and darkness is made fearful by the cracking of pistols and confused cries of strife. By day, drunkenness and debauchery are openly indulged in. The population is rotted by the foul distemper, corrupted and rendered impotent by drink, stupefied and besotted by vice. The degradation of the city folk is not only physical but mental. Tales are whispered of dark and hideous sorceries and incantations. . . ."

Layard found Mosul in a state of terror and despair, thanks to the behavior of the current pasha, or governor, of the city. This sinister individual, a Cretan-born Turk named Mohammed Keritli Oglu Pasha, was, in Layard's words, "An improved edition of Nero." Ugly and misshapen as well as thoroughly ruthless, the Pasha held Mosul in a steely grip.

"Nature had placed hypocrisy beyond his reach," Layard tells us. "He had one eye and one ear; he was short and fat, deeply marked by the small-pox, uncouth in gestures and harsh in voice." On arriving to take office at Mosul, Mohammed Pasha had sent for several of the town's leading citizens. They had fled to the country, knowing his reputation in advance, but he wheedled them back with oaths and protestations of safe-conduct, and promptly cut their throats.

Soon after, the Pasha had caused word to be spread of his death. General celebration swept the city, and Mohammed Pasha's spies noted the names of the celebrators. At midday, His Excellency appeared in the market place, in perfect health. Layard writes, "A general trembling seized the inhabitants. His vengeance fell principally upon those who possessed property, and had hitherto escaped his rapacity. They were seized and stripped, on the plea that they had spread reports detrimental to his authority."

At that time the local pashas of the Turkish Empire were allowed to fix taxes as they pleased. A certain amount had to be remitted to the Sultan; a great deal was kept for the private enrichment of the pasha; a substantial amount had to be spent by the pasha in bribes of court officials, to ensure that he continued to hold his post. Mohammed Pasha, therefore, had loosed his tax collectors on the countryside, with dismaying effect. "Go, destroy, eat!" he told them—and his agents were draining the land of money and goods.

A particularly ingenious tax invented by this ruler was the *dish-parassi*, or "tooth-money"—a tax designed to compensate a man of his rank for the wear and tear on his teeth caused by eating the coarse food of the district. This, then, was the sort of man to whom Layard presented his credentials, two days after his arrival in Mosul.

Mohammed Pasha received Layard cordially enough, "with that civility which a traveller generally expects from a Turkish functionary of high rank." The Pasha was curious as to Layard's purpose in coming to Mosul. But Layard had had ample experience with Oriental potentates by now, and he kept his goal concealed. He knew that any talk of digging up ancient palaces was sure to arouse the unsavory Pasha's greed.

To conceal his true ambitions, Layard supplied himself with a stock of guns, spears, and other weapons, and let it be known that he was going down the Tigris to hunt wild boar. On November 8, accompanied by another Englishman of Mosul and two servants, Layard engaged a raft for the five-hour river journey to the mound of Nimroud, eighteen miles to the south.

It was sunset before they arrived. Layard led the way to a nearby Arab village, which seemed ruined and deserted as he approached. They were about to return to the raft to pass the night when Layard spied the glare of a fire in a miserable hovel nearby. He saw an Arab family crouching within, around half-extinguished embers.

The head of the family, who wore the ample cloak and white turban of one of the Arab tribes settled in the district, welcomed the Europeans, and invited them to be seated. His name was Awad, and he informed Layard that his tribe, the Jehesh, had been plundered by the tax-gatherers of Mohammed Pasha, and had scattered over the countryside. Only he remained in the ruined village. Two other tribes of marauding Arabs, the Abou Salman and the Tai, were on the rampage, and the country around Nimroud was unsafe.

Seeing that Awad was intelligent and helpful, Layard told him, "I have come to dig at Nimroud, to find the palace." He offered Awad a job as superintendent of the workmen.

Awad gladly accepted. He knew the mound well, and related the traditions concerning it.

"The palace," he said, "was built by Athur, the lieutenant of Nimrod. Here the holy Abraham cast down and broke the idols of the unbelievers. The impious Nimrod, enraged at the destruction of his gods, sought to slay Abraham, and waged war against him.

"But the prophet prayed to God, and said, 'Deliver me, O God, from this man, who worships stones, and boasts himself to be the lord of all beings,' and God said to him, 'How shall I punish him?' And the prophet answered, 'To Thee armies are as nothing, and the strength and power of men likewise. Before the smallest of thy creatures will they perish.'

"And God was pleased at the faith of the prophet, and

he sent a gnat, which vexed Nimrod night and day, so that he built himself a room of glass in yonder palace, that he might dwell therein, and shut out the insect. But the gnat entered also, and passed by his ear into his brain, upon which it fed, and increased in size day by day, so that the servants of Nimrod beat his head with a hammer continually, that he might have some ease from his pain. But he died after suffering these torments for four hundred years."

Layard smiled at Awad's stories. But he did not ignore them, for he knew the Biblical reference to Nimrod, "A mighty hunter before the Lord." *Genesis* told how Nimrod's kingdom had included "Babel, and Erech, and Accad, and Calneh, in the land of Shinar"—all Sumerian and Babylonian cities—and how he had built Nineveh, and Calah, and other cities. Biblical tradition and Arab tradition coincided in giving Nimrod's name to the mound of Nimroud.

Late that night, Awad left for the village of Selamiyah, three miles away, to hire some workmen for the excavations. Layard settled down and tried to sleep. But sleep would not come. The hovel in which he lay was hardly an inviting place, but the discomfort was not what kept him awake. His fevered brain was throbbing with excitement:

"Visions of palaces underground, of gigantic monsters, of sculptured figures, and endless inscriptions, floated before me. After forming plan after plan for removing the earth, and extricating these treasures, I fancied myself wandering in a maze of chambers from which I could find no outlet. Then again, all was reburied, and I was standing on the grass-covered mound."

Finally Layard began to slip into a troubled doze. Hardly had sleep come to him when he was awakened by the voice of Awad outside the hut. Dawn had come, and Awad had returned with six Arabs who had agreed to work for a small sum.

The mound of Nimroud was twenty minutes' walk away. On Layard's last visit it had been brilliant with flowers, but now, after the long, hot summer, it was a parched waste, and sand danced swirlingly in the slanting breezes. With all vegetation dead, Layard was able to inspect the surface of the mound closely. Broken pottery and fragments of bricks were strewn everywhere. Almost every piece bore cuneiform inscriptions.

The Arabs joined the investigation. The entire group roamed the mound, stooping to pick up bits of rubbish. One Arab brought Layard a fragment of a bas-relief, which resembled in every way the burned limestone slabs of Khorsabad.

There could be no doubt that important ruins lay buried here. But where to begin? The mound was 1800 feet long, 900 wide, more than 60 feet high.

Awad pointed to a piece of alabaster jutting above the soil. No amount of tugging would pull it free, so Layard gave the orders to dig.

In a few moments it was clear that they had found the upper part of a large slab. All the workmen now were employed, and soon a second slab appeared, and a third. By mid-morning ten more had been found, forming a square —the walls of a chamber. There were no reliefs carved on the slabs, but cuneiform inscriptions covered all of them.

Leaving half his workmen to continue there, Layard moved on to the opposite side of the mound, the southwest corner, where another slab was visible. "I dug at once into the side of the mound, which was here very steep, and thus avoided the necessity of removing much earth. We came almost immediately to a wall, bearing inscriptions in the same character as those already described; but the slabs had evidently been exposed to intense heat, were cracked in every part, and, reduced to lime, threatened to fall to pieces as soon as uncovered."

Night halted the work. It had not been a wasted day. In his first few hours of excavation, Layard had had a thrill far more vivid than any *Arabian Nights* tale could provide. He had proved that he was right about Nimroud: it did contain ruined palaces of an ancient kingdom! He was convinced that he had begun to uncover the remains of the great city of Nineveh, once the pride of the blood-thirsty Assyrian kings.

The next morning, five more workmen showed up and were hired. Layard put half his men to work clearing the chamber first discovered, which he called the Northwest Palace. With the rest of the crew, he followed the wall that was emerging at the southwest corner.

Late in the day, the northwest chamber was clear, and Layard entered it, perhaps feeling like a monarch stepping within his new palace for the first time. He found himself in a room built of limestone slabs eight feet high, four to six feet wide, placed upright and close together.

Strangely, one slab bore an inscription in Arabic— the name of Ahmed Pasha, a former governor of Mosul! Startled, Layard asked his workmen for information.

One of them knew the story. "Some Christians were employed to dig into the mound about thirty years before, in search of stone for the repair of the tomb of Sultan Abd-Allah, a Mussulman saint, buried on the left bank of the Tigris. . . . They uncovered this slab; but being unable to move it, they cut upon it the name of their employer, the Pasha. My informant further stated that, in another

77

part of the mound, he had forgotten the precise spot, they had found sculptured figures, which they broke in pieces, the fragments being used in the reparation of the tomb."

In the rubbish at the bottom of the chamber Layard found some attractive ivory ornaments. Some of them bore traces of gilding. Awad, who had believed from the first that Layard was actually in search of gold, carefully gathered every bit of gold leaf he found in the rubbish, and brought it all to Layard.

Calling him aside, he whispered, "O Bey, your books are right, and the Franks know that which is hid from the true believer. Here is the gold, sure enough, and, please God, we shall find it all in a few days. Only don't say anything about it to these Arabs, for they are asses and cannot hold their tongues. The matter will come to the ears of the Pasha."

Layard was greatly amused, and to Awad's huge surprise made him a present of the scraps of gold leaf, and all such that might turn up thereafter. "He left me, muttering, 'Yia Rubbi!' and other pious ejaculations, and lost in conjectures as to the meaning of these strange proceedings."

The Northwest Palace seemed less immediately promising to Layard than the ruins at the other end of the mound. Unlike modern-day archaeologists, who carefully sift through every inch of soil, photographing and taking minute notes on everything they find, Layard was mostly interested in finding attractive sculptures to ornament the halls of the British Museum.

He transferred all his workmen to the southwest corner, and they began to dig at a rapid pace, often doing serious structural damage to the rooms and walls they unearthed. No matter. Finding sculpture was the important thing.

On November 13, after five days of work, Layard was still disappointed in his search for sculpture. He had found limestone slabs galore, and endless cuneiform inscriptions, but nothing of a pictorial nature. Leaving his men still at work, he returned to Mosul late that night, feeling that the time had come to see the Pasha and inform him of the work in progress.

Layard was fairly sure that Mohammed Pasha had already learned the truth about the "boar-hunting" expedition. At first though, the Pasha pretended to know nothing about Layard's doings at Nimroud. Finally, however, he "pulled out of his writing-tray a scrap of paper, as dingy as that produced by Awad, in which was also preserved an almost invisible particle of gold-leaf. This, he said, had been brought to him by the commander of the irregular troops stationed at Selamiyah, who had been watching my proceedings. I suggested that he should name an agent to be present as long as I worked at Nimroud, to take charge of all the precious metals that might be discovered. He promised to write on the subject to the chief of the irregulars; but offered no objection to the continuation of my researches."

Layard sensed that the Pasha was going to stir up trouble for him very shortly. Opposition to his work was coming also from an unexpected quarter—the French residents of Mosul.

The French, thrilled by Botta's success, had come to think of the Assyrian mounds as their own personal property. It annoyed them that an Englishman should have appeared and begun to dig up Nimroud. Layard and Botta had always been on the best of terms, and Botta certainly would not have had any objections to Layard's work. Botta, however, was temporarily away from Mosul, and other members of the French Consulate were less kindly disposed toward Layard. They were "not backward in throwing obstacles in my way, and in fanning the prejudices of the authorities and natives of the town."

The French acting Consul, Rouet, was Layard's particular rival. He began to send men around the countryside, "opening up mounds" wherever they could be found. This was a way of staking France's claim to them. Layard was forced to do the same, and hired men to explore several nearby mounds before the French got to them. Some of these turned out to contain ancient ruins; most were merely natural hills, or else covered medieval towns of no immediate interest to Layard.

On November 19, Layard returned to Nimroud and increased his crew to thirty men. He divided them into three groups and set them to work at the southwest corner of the mound. Deep trenches were dug; the Arabs were too weak to dig properly, and for that job Layard used Nestorians, hardy mountain men of an unusual Christian sect. The Arabs' function now was simply to haul away the earth and clear the excavated areas.

Since the Abou Salman and Tai Arabs were making the plains surrounding Nimroud unsafe, Layard decided to move his headquarters to Selamiyah, three miles away. He rented a mud hut, whose roof was too leaky to keep back much of the winter rain that was now falling. Layard spent his nights "crouched up in a corner, or under a rude table which I had constructed. The latter, having been surrounded by trenches to carry off the accumulating waters, generally afforded the best shelter."

Work continued despite the rain. On November 28, the workmen cleared away a large accumulation of earth mixed with charcoal, charred wood, and broken bricks, and entered a new chamber. The first stroke of the pick disclosed the top of a bas-relief. Sculpture at last! The Arabs were as excited as Layard, and worked until dark in torrential downpours.

The next day Layard sent a jubilant letter to his mother.

"Since I last wrote to you I have been employed like the veriest mole in grubbing up the earth, and with such success that, after having discovered several chambers built of slabs of white marble, I yesterday alighted upon sculptures resembling in character those of M. Botta's monument at Khorsabad. I have now no doubt that the whole mound of Nimroud, vast as it is, contains the ruins of one great palace [it proved to contain several] and that, if I am able to continue my excavations, I shall be richly rewarded. . . .

"The slabs I have uncovered, forming the side of a chamber, are pretty well preserved. One represents warriors fighting in chariots; another, the siege of a city; others, men on horseback; all executed with much spirit. The inscriptions already discovered are exceedingly numerous, amounting fully to one hundred, and I have been, as you may suppose, fully occupied in copying these extraordinary specimens of penmanship. I need scarcely say that they are all in the cuneiform character, very long and very complicated."

Layard's joy in finding the sculptures, unfortunately, had been dampened by a visit on the night of the twenty-eighth from Daoud Agha, captain of the Turkish troops at Selamiyah. Daoud Agha delivered himself of a long speech, to the effect that he was a servant of the Pasha, who was in turn the slave of the Sultan, and that servants were bound to obey the commands of their master.

Layard guessed what this was leading up to, and he was right. Orders had come from Mosul: the excavations were to be halted at once!

There was no point in arguing with Daoud Agha. The next morning—immediately after writing the letter to his mother quoted above—Layard saddled up and rode to town to see the Pasha.

Keritli Oglu Pasha seemed surprised to learn the news. "I gave no such order!" he declared. "I will send a letter at once to Daoud Agha, instructing him to assist you in every way!"

Layard agreed to wait in Mosul until the afternoon, when the letter could be written. But shortly an official told him that the Pasha was involved in other business. "As the Pasha was unwilling to detain me he would forward the letter in the night. I rode back to the village and acquainted Daoud Agha with the result of my visit. About midnight, however, he returned to me, and declared that a horseman had just brought him more stringent orders than any he had yet received, and that on no account was he to permit me to carry on the work."

Bewildered by these shifts and changes, Layard hurried back to Mosul. The one-eyed Pasha received him contritely, and told him, "It was with deep regret that I learned, after your departure yesterday, that the mound in which you are digging had been used as a burying-ground for Moslems, and was covered with their graves. Now you are aware that by the law it is forbidden to disturb a tomb." The Cadi and Mufti—two fanatical religious leaders of Mosul—were very disturbed over Layard's sacrilege, the Pasha declared solemnly.

Layard retorted that there were no graves at Nimroud, for one thing. For another, was the Pasha really afraid of the Cadi and Mufti, whose complaints he had ignored at other times?

The Pasha shrugged. The matter was beyond his control. "No, I cannot allow you to proceed," he told Layard. "You are my dearest and most intimate friend; if anything happens to you, what grief should I not suffer! Your life is more valuable than old stones; besides, the responsibility would fall upon my head."

There was no budging the Pasha. It seemed as though the excavations would indeed have to be halted. Layard asked for and got permission to make drawings of the sculptures already uncovered, and copies of the inscriptions. The Pasha would send an official to supervise the work.

Layard returned to Nimroud. He called a temporary halt to the digging, but kept his workmen on hand to guard the slabs that had been found. The Pasha's representative was content to remain at Selamiyah, allowing Layard to carry on a certain amount of quiet digging surreptitiously.

The day after his return, Layard rode out to the mound to have a look at the so-called Moslem graves he was accused of desecrating, and which he knew did not exist. To his surprise, he found that grave-markers now rose at Nimroud, where they had not been a few days before!

Daoud Agha cheerfully confessed what had happened. The Turkish officer admitted that he and his troops had been busy for the last two nights, hauling gravestones from distant villages to place them at Nimroud. "We have destroyed more real tombs of the true Believers," Daoud Agha said, "in making sham ones, than you could have defiled between the Zab and Selamiyah. We have killed our horses and ourselves in carrying those accursed stones."

The situation was at once funny and grim. Layard knew that he had powerful enemies in Mosul. Not only were the Moslem leaders opposed to him, but he had good reason to think that the French of Mosul had helped to stir up this latest trick.

On the sly, Layard and a few men opened a couple of new trenches. The results were gratifying. "Near the western edge we came upon the lower part of several gigantic creatures. . . . At the foot of the S.E. corner was found a crouching lion, rudely carved in basalt, which appeared to have fallen from the building above, and to have been exposed for centuries to the atmosphere. In the center of the mound we uncovered part of a pair of gigantic winged bulls, the head and half the wings of which had been destroyed."

These bulls had been carved in high relief on the backs of enormous alabaster slabs fourteen feet long and almost as high. Near them was a pair of small winged lions carved in the same manner, and a human figure nine feet high, in stunningly high relief.

Layard did not trouble himself to uncover any of these reliefs completely at this point. He was satisfied to prove their existence. He did not want to lay them bare and expose them to the risk of injury while matters were still so uncertain.

The end of the year was approaching. Layard sent word to Sir Stratford Canning of his exciting discoveries, and also of his troubles with the Pasha. What was needed, Layard wrote, was a *firman* from the Sultan, authorizing him in writing to excavate without interference from the local authorities.

Without this, Layard knew he could not proceed. Daoud Agha agreed to remove the false "graves" from

Nimroud, and Layard in turn covered over the sculptures he had found, and withdrew from Nimroud.

Entering Mosul on December 18, Layard found the city in a state of wild glee. Word had come from Constantinople that morning that the Sultan, having received an account of Mohammed Pasha's behavior, had removed the one-eyed Cretan from office. A liberal-minded young Turkish general named Ismail Pasha would govern the town until the new permanent governor, Hafiz Pasha, could arrive. Ismail Pasha's reputation for tolerance and justice delighted the suffering people of Mosul.

The new governor had already taken office. A British consular official had called on the deposed Mohammed Pasha that morning and found him in a dilapidated hovel through which the rain poured freely. "Thus it is with God's creatures," the ex-Pasha muttered. "Yesterday all those dogs were kissing my feet; today everyone and everything falls upon me, even the rain!"

Layard could hardly grieve at his enemy's downfall. But he decided not to resume his excavations just yet. He resolved instead to go to Baghdad, where he could make arrangements for the eventual shipment of his finds to England, and where he could consult with several experts on the ancient world who happened to be in that city just then.

He hired a raft, and floated off down the Tigris. He was in Baghdad by Christmas Eve.

VIII

WINGED BULLS AND BEARDED KINGS

Back in Mosul early in January, Layard found the city prospering under Ismail Pasha's wise rule. Layard called on the new governor, who had no objections to the resumption of his operations at Nimroud.

During Layard's absence his Nestorian workmen had been busy, investigating on their own. A mound called Baasheikha had yielded pottery, bricks and fragments of sculpture. Another mound, Karamles, proved to contain a brick platform, and the bricks were stamped with cuneiform. Layard's familiarity with cuneiform had grown so that he could now recognize, though not translate, the names of kings. The Karamles bricks bore the same royal name as the bricks Botta had found at Khorsabad.

Nimroud was green with new grass. The black tents of the Arabs now dotted the plain, since the Abou Salman tribe, reassured by the good wishes of the new Pasha, had given up their looting and were again pasturing their herds near Nimroud. Awad's tribe, the Jehesh, had also returned to their village and were busy with the spring planting. "Even on the mound the plough opened its furrows, and corn was sown over the palaces of the Assyrian kings," Layard writes.

With everything so suddenly tranquil, Layard was able to move his headquarters back from Selamiyah to Nimroud itself. He hired three huts for himself and his staff. Hormuzd Rassam, the brother of the British Vice-Consul, came to live with him and to handle some of the details of the work, such as distributing the payments to the work-men.

The last of the counterfeit graves were removed from the mound—along with some genuine ones that turned up. Layard's Arab workmen were a little troubled at uprooting these, but he convinced them that, since the bodies were not turned toward Mecca, they could not be those of true believers. Nevertheless he ordered the remains to be carefully reburied at the foot of the mound.

Resuming the excavations, Layard almost at once ran into a new snag: the Cadi, that bigoted religious leader of Mosul, began to agitate against him. "He is carrying away treasure that belongs to us," the Cadi declared. "And, far worse, he is finding inscriptions that proved that the Franks once held the country. They will try to conquer it again, and exterminate all true believers!"

With this sort of gossip circulating, Layard's workmen were disturbed about continuing. There was muttering in the town, and the possibility of danger for Layard. He visited Ismail Pasha, and the governor, while admitting there was no truth in the Cadi's accusations, asked Layard to suspend operations again for a while until matters calmed.

Layard took advantage of this latest delay to establish friendly relations with the sheikh of the Abou Salman Arabs, who were camped around Nimroud and who had something of a reputation for mischief. Layard brought presents to the sheikh—a silk gown and a supply of coffee and sugar—and it was agreed that Abou Salman would cause no trouble for Layard and his excavators. "We are now friends," the sheikh told Layard.

By mid-February, 1846, Layard felt it was safe to begin digging again. Each day brought new discoveries, and he was delighted by the richness of the mound. But Layard was starting to feel a financial pinch. The workmen had to be paid—not much, true, but it added up—and the slim funds with which he had begun were rapidly dwindling. Layard's great hope was that the British Museum would subsidize his work.

Almost daily, new wonders came forth. Layard was particularly struck by portraits in high relief that could only have been those of Assyrian kings—formidable, terrifying figures shown always in profile, hawk-nosed and fierce, with great curling beards descending in ringlets, and with every muscle of their legs and arms shown in astonishing detail. Other slabs showed similar figures whose heads were those of vultures.

Early in March came the most impressive discovery thus far. Layard was returning to Nimroud from the Abou Salman encampment when two Arabs came rushing up to him, breathless after a wild ride from the mound.

"Hasten, O Bey!" they called to him. "Hasten to the diggers, for they have found Nimrod himself! Wallah, it is wonderful, but it is true! We have seen him with our own eyes. There is no God but God!"

Layard hurried to the ruins and entered the new trench. The workmen, standing by in awe, were silent. Awad advanced, and asked for a present to celebrate the occasion, while the Arabs removed a screen they had built to hide the figure they had found.

An enormous alabaster head rose from the ground. It was well preserved, its features calm and majestic. Layard saw at once that it belonged to a winged bull-figure of the type Botta had found at Khorsabad.

"I was not surprised," he writes, "that the Arabs had been amazed and terrified at this apparition. It required no stretch of the imagination to conjure up the most strange fancies."

Awad told Layard that one of the workmen had, at first sight of the monster, run off in terror toward Mosul. Layard received the news sadly, for it promised trouble.

He gave orders for the rest of the earth to be cleared from the statue. Sheikh Abd-ur-Rahman of the Abou Salman arrived while this was going on, and descended into the trench to view the huge head.

"This is not the work of man's hands," he exclaimed in awe. "It was fashioned by those infidel giants of whom Mohammed, peace be with him! has said, that they were higher than the tallest date tree. This is one of the idols which Noah, peace be with him! cursed before the flood."

Layard suspected that a twin figure might be found nearby. He had a trench dug south of the head, and before nightfall found the second statue, only twelve feet away. Leaving a few men to guard the colossi, he returned to the village to celebrate the discovery.

As he had feared, news had reached Mosul—in garbled form. The Cadi of Mosul was of the opinion that the very bones of Nimrod had been uncovered, and that further digging would be sacrilege. Ismail Pasha sent word that nothing else was to be done until he could visit the excavations himself. He arrived; and, seeing that nothing but statues had been found, gave Layard permission to resume work.

He had the bulls cleared, and by the end of March had found a pair of winged human-headed lions, about twelve feet high and the same in length. Like the bulls, the lions were carved in high relief on thick stone slabs. He wrote his mother, "Nothing so beautiful as these lions was discovered by the French. . . . The lions lastly discovered are admirably drawn, and the muscles, bones, and veins quite true to nature, and portrayed with great spirit. . . . The human head, too, is really grand. It is curious that the artist has given the animal five legs. He has done this in order that, whether you look at him in front or at the side, he may appear to have the proper number; for although the figure is in relief, yet at the end of the slab it is in full. Between the legs are long inscriptions in the cuneiform character."

When he was not supervising the excavations, Layard was puzzling over the cuneiform inscriptions. His progress was slight, but he had discovered—without being able to decipher them—the names of cities and of kings, and the ends of a few words. He was assisted in this by Major Henry Rawlinson, a British soldier stationed at Baghdad, whose chief hobby was the study of cuneiform.

Spring was now at its height. The pastures were aglow with flowers, and Layard describes how his two pet greyhounds, returning from their hunting, "issued from the long grass dyed red, yellow, or blue, according to the flowers through which they had last forced their way." It was a time of festivals among the Arabs, of gaiety and relaxation. Layard had left his cramped hut in the village, which was infested with vermin, and camped now in a tent at the edge of a large pond in the plain of Nimroud.

The work continued in these pleasant surroundings. Summer drew near, and the heat mounted. Daily temperatures of 100 degrees were common by late May. Ismail Pasha turned Mosul over to the new governor, Hafiz Pasha, but he remained only a few weeks before going on to a more important post. The new governor—the fourth in the seven months Layard had been there—was Tahyar

Pasha, who luckily was sympathetic to Layard and encouraged his work in every way.

Living in a tent was no longer possible in the increasing heat, and returning to the vermin-ridden village was equally undesirable. Layard had a little cabin built out of reeds and boughs, along a bank of the Tigris, and lived there. It was cool enough, all things considered. But he was greatly troubled by what he calls "scorpions and other reptiles, which issued from the earth forming the walls of my apartment," and by the gnats and sandflies which hovered over the river.

Hot winds, coming in from the desert, burned away the lovely vegetation of the plain almost in a single day. The sky was dark with locusts, which devoured any growing plant that survived the heat. Whirlwinds struck frequently, bringing clouds of sand and dust. One day Layard's shacks at the mound were swept away by the wind, and he had to crouch for refuge behind one of his alabaster lions.

A remarkable relief turned up in May: a lengthy slab showing an Assyrian king hunting lions. Layard found it a tremendously exciting work of art. It showed the king standing in a chariot, directing an arrow at a roaring lion just a few feet behind him. A second lion, riddled with arrows, was sinking in death alongside the chariot, and the king's noble horses pranced in regal majesty.

Soon after this discovery, Layard received a welcome and long-overdue document. Sir Stratford Canning had obtained for him a *firman* from the Sultan, permitting him the right to excavate near Mosul and to remove such objects as might be discovered.

Despite the *firman*, Layard had to bring his work to a temporary halt once again. The full onset of summer made digging impossible. As he wrote to his aunt, "The Arabs can hardly stand the digging, though accustomed to the climate, and I am compelled to release them for three hours during the middle of the day. It is no joke, I can assure, to draw with the thermometer at 115, and even 117, in the shade."

He returned to Mosul to show his *firman* to the governor. Since the weather was not yet so ferocious there, Layard resolved to have a go at the mound of Kouyunjik, which Botta had sampled without much success in 1842. He put men to work at the highest part of the mound, on the southern face.

Trouble arose at once. Botta was gone, and the new French Consul, Rouet, claimed Kouyunjik as French property. His basis for this was the fact that Botta had begun to dig there four years before.

Layard refused to abide by this. Botta had, after all, given up. France had no permanent claim to the mound, which, in any event, was Turkish property to begin with. Ignoring Rouet's protests, Layard continued to work.

Feeling he had to do something to protect France's rights, Rouet hired workmen and began to dig at Kouyunjik too, nearby but carrying his trenches in the opposite direction. Thus the people of Mosul were treated to the silly spectacle of Rouet and Layard supervising simultaneous excavations a few feet apart, glaring at each other angrily all the while!

Through some sort of poetic justice, neither of them found anything but rubbish. Within a month, the heat forced both parties to quit work, nothing accomplished.

Layard's next task was to pack up the treasures he had unearthed at Nimroud, and get them on their way to England. The trip would have to be a roundabout one: down the Tigris by raft to Baghdad, then by ship to Basra, thence to Bombay and around the Cape of Good Hope to England. There was no practicable way of getting the sculptures to Constantinople for a voyage to England via the Mediterranean, and the Bombay route was only alternative.

Moving everything was a staggering task. Layard had no tractors, no bulldozers, no machinery of any sort, of course. He was faced with the problem of moving immense blocks of stone, some nearly nine feet square and a foot thick, fragile and covered with delicate sculpture. The lack of machinery was bad enough; he didn't even have access to a supply of rope strong enough to bear the weight!

Layard's solution brings shivers to modern archaeologists who regard it as sacrilege to tamper with any ancient work of art. To reduce the weight of his slabs, he simply cut away as much of their limestone backs as he could. "The inscriptions being mere repetitions," he tells us, "I did not consider it necessary to preserve them, as they added to the weight."

Using levers of wood, and by digging away the brick walls behind the slabs, he was able to haul them from the trenches. He did not at that time try to move any of the ponderous winged bulls or lions. The sawn-down slabs were packed in felts and matting, and screwed down in roughly made wooden cases. The Pasha supplied Layard with buffalo carts, upon which the cases, twelve in all, were carried down to the river and put upon rafts. The job took twenty days, under a blazing sun.

A curious kind of race developed at this point. The French at Khorsabad had not hurried to pack up their own finds for shipment to the Louvre, and they had only now reached Baghdad. A French vessel, *Le Cormoran*, was waiting at Basra for them. Layard hoped that his own cases would reach the sea first, and that London would have a collection of Assyrian sculpture ahead of Paris!

Alas for such vain hopes, it seemed to take forever for Layard's twelve packing cases to get down the river to Baghdad and then over to Basra. Nearly a year went by before they finally reached England, and by that time the Parisians had had ample opportunity to marvel over M. Botta's finds.

With the first shipment safely off, Layard closed up his Nimroud headquarters for the summer and went back to Mosul. He could not resist doing a little more digging there, in some mounds north of the city. He at once discovered a vast gateway, flanked by two winged figures even more gigantic than any he had seen before. He did not follow up his work there, and later archaeologists believed that the two great figures had been destroyed. But in 1941 a heavy rainstorm peeled away the soil and revealed them again—one complete bull and part of another—and they can be seen to this day just outside Mosul.

In August, the irrepressible Layard sneaked back to Nimroud to try to resume work. He found a few more sculptured slabs of the type that was now so pleasantly familiar, but the heat forced a complete shutdown this time. His health had been weakened by the fierce climate, and he decided to visit the Tiyari Mountains inhabited by the Nestorian Christians, and not to return to the lowlands until the heat was gone.

He departed on August 28, accompanied by Hormuzd Rassam and an odd assortment of hangers-on and followers, including two Albanian soldiers, a Turk named Ibrahim Agha, some servants, and a drunken, half-witted Nestorian named Ionunco, who would serve as guide.

On his way to the mountains, Layard stopped off at Khorsabad, fourteen miles northeast of Mosul, to see what the French were up to there. He discovered that the entire native village that topped the mound had been bought by the French government and removed. The town had been rebuilt in the plain at the foot of the mound, and Layard found nearly all the villagers suffering from malaria, since they now lived in a marshy swamp.

The French excavators, he saw, had worked much as he had, cutting trenches through the mound. The palace resembled the ones he had found at Nimroud, though the corridors were narrower and the rooms smaller in size, but higher. There is a trace of pride in his writing as he tells us that the winged bulls of Khorsabad have "an awkward and unsightly appearance," compared with those of Nimroud. And, he notes, "since M. Botta's departure the chambers had been partly filled up by the falling in of the trenches; the sculptures were rapidly perishing; and, shortly, little will remain of this remarkable monument."

He left Khorsabad quickly to avoid coming down with the fever and headed for the mountains. Now began a long, fascinating journey through the mountain-country. When he had visited the Persian mountaineers years before, Layard had traveled alone, dependent on the mercy of anyone he met. Now he proceeded with a large retinue, and his fame went before him. Although he was only 29, he had become an important personage in the Orient. He was received warmly everywhere and was exposed to none of the dangers that beset him on his earlier travels.

He visited the Nestorians, who had recently been the victims of an atrocious massacre perpetrated by the unruly Kurdish mountaineers. Layard later wrote a detailed and lengthy account of Nestorian life and customs.

He visited the Kurds as well, and also an odd sect called the Yezidis, who were regarded as devil-worshippers by most of the other peoples of the region. Layard found the Yezidis likable and honest, and reported that their curious religion was not at all a form of devil-worship, all rumor to the contrary. Layard spent a great deal of time among them, returning to Mosul in October, impatient now to begin digging again.

IX

PROBLEMS AND PLEASURES

News from England was waiting for him. Sir Stratford Canning had displayed Layard's letters and drawings in London, and the British Museum had agreed to grant funds for further work.

It was good news, but nothing to be really joyful over. The museum offered him only a small sum, not at all equivalent to the generous grants Botta had received from France. Layard was dismayed. Was Britain really so stingy? Didn't people realize the importance of these finds?

It did not appear that way. Whereas Botta had been lavishly supplied with money and reimbursed for every expense, Layard was told to scrape along on a pittance. Unhappily, he realized he would have to change the nature of his work. His purpose now was "To obtain the largest possible number of well-preserved objects of art at the least possible outlay of money."

This was not exactly an ideal goal. Archaeology should be carried out slowly and with the greatest of care. Once damage has been done, it can never be undone, and the archaeologist must answer to his own conscience. As one of the greatest of modern archaeologists, Sir Leonard Woolley, puts it, "All excavation is destruction. The archaeologist unearths a building, perhaps removing two or three later constructions in order to do so; its walls remain and can be seen, or, if the wind-blown sand covers them again, they can be dug out a second time, but all the evidence given by stratification, by the position of objects, by the traces of wood ash or by fallen brickwork, this has gone, and can never be recovered . . . any evidence that he has failed to note has gone forever, and unless his record is scientifically complete he has defrauded science, and had better not have dug at all."

This methodical approach did not come into general use until the beginning of the twentieth century. All too many zealous archaeologists of the old school did terrible damage, and Layard was among them.

Layard was aware of his shortcomings. He blamed his lack of funds, saying, "Few of the chambers were fully explored, and many small objects of great interest may have been left undiscovered." He was saddened, too, by the way much of what he found suffered from exposure to the air. The methods of preservation that archaeologists use today simply did not exist in 1846, and Layard did not have the funds to use even such techniques as were available to him.

"Many of the sculptures and monuments discovered," he writes unhappily, "were in too dilapidated a condition to be removed, and others threatened to fall to pieces as soon as uncovered." He longed for an artist, like Botta's Flandin, who would make a record of the works of art before they vanished forever. But England could not manage to afford an artist.

"I made up my mind to do the best I could; to copy as carefully and accurately as possible, that which I saw before me." As he admitted, "I had neither knowledge nor experience as a draftsman, but that could not be helped. "I had therefore to superintend the excavations; to draw all the bas-reliefs discovered; to copy and compare the innumerable inscriptions; to take casts of them; and to preside over the moving and packing of the sculptures. As there was no one whom I could trust to overlook the diggers, I was obliged to be continually present, and frequently to remove the earth myself from the face of the slabs—as, through the carelessness and inexperience of the workmen, they were exposed to injury from the blows of the picks."

By November 1, Layard was digging at Nimroud again. He had a fairly large group of workmen now. They were divided into groups consisting of two or four Nestorian diggers, and eight or ten Arabs who carried the dirt away. Since the British Museum had instructed Layard to bury the building with earth after he had explored it, he had each chamber filled with earth taken from the next, first, of course, copying all inscriptions and drawing the sculptures.

Layard now began to find delicate objects of ivory, copper, iron, and even glass. His account takes on a melancholy tone as he tells us how fragile everything was. Again and again, we read paragraphs like this:

"Several helmets of other shapes, some with the arched crest, were also uncovered; but they fell to pieces as soon as exposed; and I was only able, with the greatest care, to gather up a few of the fragments which still held together, for the iron was in so complete a state of decomposition that it crumbled away on being touched."

It becomes a heartbreaking refrain: ". . . when the rubbish was cleared away it was perfect, but immediately fell to pieces . . . copper vessels of peculiar shape . . . fell to pieces almost immediately on exposure to the air, and I was unable to preserve one of them. . . ."

Painted frescoes on the wall suffered too: "The plaster

fell from the walls in flakes, notwithstanding all my efforts to preserve it. . . ." Ivories, we read, "on their discovery fell to pieces almost upon mere exposure to the air. . . ." And, Layard adds, "A workman . . . came upon a perfect vase; but unfortunately struck it with his pick, and broke away the upper part of it. . . ."

A remarkable discovery was waiting for him in the center of the mound, where the first two huge winged bulls had been found. Reasoning that the bulls had been flankers for a gate, Layard had his men search for the wall that must have surrounded them. More slabs turned up, and fragments of a crudely done winged bull. The new trench ran fifty feet. Layard was ready to abandon it when the corner of a polished black stone appeared, ten feet below the surface.

It was cleared and hauled from the ruins, and Layard saw that he had a masterpiece. It was an obelisk of black marble, with sculptured reliefs on all four sides, and an inscription 210 lines in length. The reliefs showed a king, with a prisoner at his feet, and a procession of men approaching him leading various animals—elephants, rhinoceroses, camels, monkeys—and bringing tribute.

The obelisk was quickly copied, packed, and sent off to Baghdad for shipment to England. If Layard had been able to read the lengthy inscription on his obelisk, his delight would have been boundless. For he had found an unquestionable and solid link between Assyria and the world of the Old Testament. The king shown on the obelisk, we now know, was Shalmaneser III (858–824 B.C.), and one of those shown paying tribute to him was Jehu, King of Israel.

Layard was still thwarted in his attempts to decipher Assyrian cuneiform writing. He had been able to work out the relationships between three kings, but their names remained unknown to him, and we find him still speaking of "the Khorsabad king" and "the son of the builder of the Northwest Palace." He had decided that the son of the Khorsabad king had built one of the palaces in the mound of Kouyunjik, and that *his* son had been the builder of the Northwest Palace at Nimroud. Amazingly, Layard's guesses were almost right, as later scholars found.

Layard found that not only was he responsible for paying his workmen, he also had to maintain law and order among them. They appointed him as a kind of judge, since he demanded no bribes for settling disputes, unlike the regular local officials. He decided property disputes, quarrels over women, breaches of contract, and all manner of other disagreements—probably wishing he had studied his lawbooks a little more diligently ten years before.

By December he had enough sculpture to send a second cargo to Baghdad. He purchased materials for building a large raft, and mats and felts for packing his treasures. These things came down from Mosul, but his Arab boatmen were robbed during the night and the mats and felts stolen.

It took him three days to find the culprits. They were Arabs camped in the Nimroud plain, and were notorious for their thieving ways. Accompanied by several of his men, Layard set off for the camp at dawn and approached the sheikh.

"Peace be with you!" Layard began. "Your health and spirits are, please God, good. We have long been friends, although it has never yet been my good fortune to see you. I know the laws of friendship; that which is my property is your property, and the contrary. But there are a few things, such as mats, felts, and ropes, which come from afar, and are very necessary to me, whilst they can be of little use to you; otherwise God forbid that I should ask for them. You will greatly oblige me by giving these things to me."

The sheikh's reply was just as courtly. "As I am your sacrifice, O Bey, no such things as mats, felts, or ropes were ever in my tents. Search, and if such things be found we give them to you willingly."

"Wallah, the Sheikh has spoken the truth," exclaimed the tribe.

"That is exactly what I want to ascertain," Layard declared, noticing one of his precious ropes supporting the tentpole. "And, as this is a matter of doubt, the Pasha must decide between us."

Layard gave a signal. One of his men stepped forward on cue and snapped a pair of handcuffs on the astonished sheikh, and, jumping on his horse, dragged the Arab out of the tent.

Smiling, Layard mounted his own horse at a leisurely pace. "Now," he said to the dumfounded Arabs, "I have found a part of that which I wanted; you must search for the rest."

The Arabs were well armed, but their Sheikh was a prisoner, and they made no hostile moves. Layard brought his captive to Nimroud, and regaled him with stories of the tortures that the Pasha of Mosul would undoubtedly inflict on him. Soon the unhappy Arab confessed the theft, and the next morning the stolen goods were returned, with a lamb and a kid by way of a peace-offering.

By the middle of December, a second cargo of sculptures was ready to be sent to Baghdad. Layard notes, "I was again obliged to have recourse to the buffalo-carts of the Pasha; and as none of the bas-reliefs and objects to be moved were of great weight, these rotten and unwieldy vehicles could be patched up for the occasion. On Christmas day I had the satisfaction of seeing a raft, bearing twenty-three cases, in one of which was the obelisk, floating down the river. I watched them until they were out of sight, and then galloped into Mosul to celebrate the festivities of the season, with the few Europeans whom duty or business had collected in this remote corner of the globe."

While he was at Mosul, Layard's hot temper got the better of him again, and nearly put a finish to his career in Mesopotamia. He was investigating Kouyunjik again, taking a ferry across the Tigris and back every day. One day he remained at the mound so late that all the ferrymen had gone home but one. Layard got to him just in time, and hired him.

Layard's workmen and overseers boarded the ferry. Two Turkish soldiers appeared and asked to be allowed to cross, and Layard sent them aboard. The ferry had just pushed off when Layard noticed a party of men on foot hurrying toward the river. "Thinking they were travelers, and that they would have to remain out for the night unless I gave them a passage, I ordered the boatmen to return to the shore, and to wait for them. When they arrived, I found that the party consisted of the Cadi of Mosul and his attendants, who were coming from Nebbi Yunus, the so-called tomb of Jonah."

The Cadi, that dour, fanatical son of Islam, was one of Layard's most dedicated enemies in Mosul. Despite this, Layard invited him politely enough to come aboard, and the Cadi eagerly accepted.

The ferry was a crude boat with a pointed prow rising

high at one end, and a lofty poop on which stood the steersman. There was room for only one other person on this poop, and the rest of the passengers had to crowd together in the deep, spacious, and dirty hull of the vessel.

Layard had customarily taken the position next to the steersman, and he took it now, with the Cadi standing just beneath him. This seemed to offend the Cadi. When the ferry was midway across the river, then half a mile wide and running dangerously fast, the Cadi suddenly shook his fist at Layard and cried out, "Shall the dogs occupy the high places, whilst the true believers have to stand below?" He added some choice curses aimed at Christians in general.

Religious intolerance had never been easy for Layard to accept. He was particularly annoyed that the Cadi would return his generosity with curses. Losing his temper, he lashed out with a short hooked stick that he was carrying. The Cadi was wearing a thick turban, and Layard did not think that the blow would have much effect. To his surprise and distress he saw blood begin to stream down the Cadi's face.

The Cadi's followers drew their swords and pistols. The two Turkish soldiers quickly rushed to Layard's protection. Layard himself, jumping down into the lower part of the boat, seized the Cadi by the throat.

"I'll throw him overboard if anyone attacks me," Layard announced.

No one moved. The ferry reached the other shore with Layard still gripping the Cadi.

As soon as they had landed, the Cadi, blood still on his face, entered Mosul and proclaimed loudly that he had been assaulted and beaten by a *Giaour*—an infidel—and that Mohammed and his faith had been insulted. There was an immediate uproar and commotion. An ugly crowd gathered. It was altogether possible that there might be a massacre of Christians.

Layard hurried to the Pasha to explain what had happened, ordered him in a rather lordly way to take precautions for the safety of all Europeans in Mosul, "and warned him that he would be held responsible by the British Government, and by the Ambassador at Constantinople, for anything that might happen to me."

Luckily, the Pasha and the Cadi were bitter enemies themselves. The Pasha, instead of upbraiding Layard, "denounced the Cadi as an ill-conditioned fellow in no very complimentary terms, and declared that he had been rightly punished for the insult of which he had been guilty." The town police were ordered to be alert for any anti-Christian demonstrations. The Pasha suggested that Layard remain at the governor's residence until the hubbub blew over.

Layard refused. He mounted his horse and rode boldly through the streets to his residence. Angry and menacing looks came his way, but nobody attempted to molest him.

For a few days the situation was tense. Layard was asked to leave town until matters calmed, but declined to do so, and went every day to the Tigris and across to Kouyunjik. The Cadi filed a protest with the Sultan, who in time passed it along to Sir Stratford Canning. Sir Stratford took no action, other than to beg Layard to be more cautious with his fists in the future. Gradually the matter was forgotten, after an uneasy week of tension.

A little later that winter, Layard ventured downriver to the mound of Qalah Shergat, a good distance south of

Nimroud. His one major find there was a damaged life-sized statue in black basalt—not a relief—of a headless royal figure. Though so badly weathered that it was of little artistic value, the statue was important in that it was the first Assyrian statue in the round that had been found. Only a handful of such works have ever been found, to this day. The Qalah Shergat figure has been identified as Shalmaneser III, the king also shown on the black obelisk of Nimroud.

Layard was puzzled to find almost nothing else of interest in the mound. There was no alabaster, none of the stonework so common to the north. Since there were no stone-quarries in the vicinity of Qalah Shergat, Layard guessed that "unbaked bricks alone may have been used; and if so, the walls built with them could no longer, without very careful examination, be distinguished from the soil in which they are buried."

Once again Layard was quite right. More than half a century later, German archaeologists came to work at Qalah Shergat. They identified the mound as the site of Assur, the earliest Assyrian capital. Trained in the newest techniques, the Germans were able—as Layard was not —to distinguish between mud-brick walls and surrounding debris. Assur's walls and palaces were of brick and not of stone. Layard, as a pioneer, simply did not have the techniques needed to cope with such a challenge. He abandoned work at Qalah Shergat after a few days.

The rains of winter gave way to the flowers of spring. A friend of Layard's from Constantinople, his one-time roommate there, Mr. Longworth, came to inspect the diggings at Nimroud. Longworth had succeeded Layard as correspondent for the *Morning Post*, and he sent back to England a glowing report on Layard's work which, published in the spring of 1847, must have caused a stir of excitement there.

Word came, too, of Layard's first literary honor. While at Baghdad in 1842, recovering from fever and fatigue, he had written a paper on his wanderings in the Bakhtiyari country of Persia. This had been published in the *Journal of the Royal Geographical Society* for 1846. Now, the Society had decided to award a gold medal to Layard in token of the excellence of his article.

By the end of April 1847 Layard was ready to take stock of his work at Nimroud and start to wind it up for the summer. He had every reason to feel pleased with himself. In the Northwest Palace alone, he had explored twenty-eight halls and chambers, most of them lined with sculptured slabs. He had found thirteen pairs of gigantic winged bulls and lions, and had sent thirty-five cases of antiquities to England.

As the hot weather drew near, he began to assemble his third shipment of packing-cases—more than thirty in all. Anything not included in that shipment would simply have to be re-buried until some later time. One omission troubled Layard. He had sent a great deal to England, but had not included any of the winged colossi. He wanted to send one of the giant bulls, and one of the lions.

But how? It seemed impossible. Impossible, that is, for anyone but Layard.

X

A BULL TO THE RIVER

Botta had found bulls of great size at Khorsabad, too. The Frenchman had hoped to ship them to Paris, and had built a cart with wheels a yard thick. A gang of six hundred workmen had attempted to drag a monumental bull across the fifteen miles of farmland that separated Khorsabad from the river.

The attempt had failed. The wheels bogged down halfway. Botta was forced to saw his vast bulls up into manageable sections, which were shipped to Paris in crates and glued together at the Louvre. The British Museum had instructed Layard not to do the same, but to leave the bulls where they were until some way of bringing them to England whole could be devised.

Layard was determined to outdo the French. He would bring back a bull, and a winged lion too! He picked out the best of his bulls and the finest of his lions, and arranged for a cart to be built to transport them.

There was no wood in Mosul strong enough to bear such weights. Layard sent carpenters to the mountains to find sturdy mulberry planks. The French Consulate, for once cooperative, loaned Layard the strong iron axles that Botta had used in his attempt to move bulls. A good-sized four-wheeled cart was constructed. Mosul had never seen anything like it before, and crowds gathered in front of Vice-Consul Rassam's house, where the great cart had been assembled. When word spread that the cart was going to be taken to the river to be floated on a raft to Nimroud, the entire business of the town halted, and everyone came out to view the spectacle.

The bull and lion had been carved as reliefs against blocks of limestone ten feet square. To lessen their weight, Layard had the slabs cut away in back, justifying his action by remarking, "as the back of the slab was never meant to be seen, being placed against the wall of sun-dried bricks, no part of the sculpture was sacrificed." Even so, they weighed some ten tons apiece.

In order to get the bull from the mound to the plain below, it was necessary to cut a trench some 200 feet long, 15 feet wide, and, in some places, 20 feet deep. Fifty workmen were needed for this job, and while they were cutting the trench they came upon some new chambers and more sculptured slabs, and also the main sewer of the palace.

Layard's plan was to tip the bull from its standing position over onto its back, letting the unsculptured side of the slab rest on rollers. To manage this, he cut away the walls behind it. The problem was to lower it. Once safely onto its cart, sheer brute force would probably suffice to haul the bull to the river. But how to tip the bull from vertical to horizontal without losing control and letting it smash?

He proposed to anchor it with ropes as it descended. Mosul rope was worthless, but he got thick palm-fiber hawsers from Baghdad. To prevent injury in case of a fall, and to keep the ropes themselves from chipping or rubbing the stone, Layard swathed the bull in mats and felts.

All was ready for the great attempt, finally. The bull stood supported by wooden props. Rollers, well-greased, were ready to receive the vast weight. Layard had contrived an elaborate block and tackle arrangement, passing ropes around the bull and anchoring them through two nearby blocks of stone. The ends of the ropes were given to two groups of strong men. The idea was that while one group of workmen gradually removed the wooden props holding the bull up, the others would pay out the rope, slowly allowing the big sculpture to tip on its side and descend to the rollers.

A crowd was on hand to watch and help—the whole populations of several of the nearby villages, and Sheikh Abd-ur-Rahman and his tribe of Arabs. Layard stationed himself on a high bank of earth atop a second bull, deploying his workmen at the ropes and at the props.

He gave the word: "Start removing the props!"

The bull remained in its place as the wedges were knocked away. A rope was passed around it, and six or seven workmen tugged. The bull began to tilt. The other cable supporting it started to stretch with the strain, but it held.

Slowly, agonizingly, the bull descended. Struggling gangs of workmen hauled on the main rope to keep the big slab from falling and shattering. Nestorian workmen, risking their lives, darted under the tipping bull to insert new props of wood and to remove the old ones, changing the angle of the bull. Some of the watchers had brought drums and shrill pipes, which now sounded, adding to the tension of the moment.

Layard writes, "The Arabs were half frantic with excitement. They had thrown off nearly all their garments: their long hair floated in the wind; and they indulged in the wildest postures and gesticulations as they clung to the ropes. The women had congregated on the sides of their trenches, and by their incessant, ear-piercing screams, added to the enthusiasm of the men."

Layard's own instructions were drowned out in the din. He scooped up clods of earth and threw them at the noisiest of the Arabs, trying to silence them. To no avail. The bull continued to descend. As it came closer to the ground, it was no longer possible to insert new props. The cable had to bear the entire strain. The dry ropes creaked and gave off clouds of dust.

"Throw water on them!" Layard bellowed.

Before anyone could do anything, the cable parted with the bull still five feet from the rollers. Down it crashed, and the men who had been tugging on the cable went flying backwards, heels over head!

Grimly, Layard vaulted into the trench, expecting to find the bull in fragments. He was delighted to find it was still in one piece—and that it had landed exactly where he had wished to put it.

The Arabs split the air with new cries of glee. The musicians pounded their drums and puffed out their cheeks to sound their pipes. A wild dance of joy began.

Layard waited until everyone was calm again. Then he began the laborious process of dragging the bull out of the trench. Cables were fixed to the rollers, and the workmen hauled it forward. The sun was going down, now, and there was little point in trying to finish the job that day. "The Arabs dressed themselves," Layard writes, "and placing the musicians at their head, marched toward the village, singing their war-songs, and occasionally raising a wild yell, throwing their lances into the air, and flourishing their swords and shields over their heads."

Layard rode with them. Playful Arab horsemen pranced about him, pretending to menace him with their lances. Layard was a little uncomfortable, knowing that if a horse stumbled he would be spitted there and then. But the demonstration was meant as a compliment, and allowed the young warriors to show off their prowess as horsemen. Shrugging away his fears, Layard declared he was delighted at the show, and praised everyone.

At the Arab camp, Sheikh Abd-ur-Rahman was overcome with awe. "Wonderful! Wonderful!" he cried. "There is no god but God, and Mohammed is his prophet!"

As they feasted by the fire, the Sheikh asked Layard, "In the name of the Most High, O Bey, what are you going to do with those stones. So many thousands of purses spent upon such things! Can it be, as you say, that your people learn wisdom from them; or is it, as his reverence the Cadi declares, that they are to go to the palace of your Queen, who, with the rest of the unbelievers, worships these idols?"

Layard smiled. He had long ago given up trying to combat the malicious tales spread by His Reverence the Cadi.

Sheikh Abd-ur-Rahman went on: "As for wisdom, these figures will not teach you to make any better knives or scissors; and it is in the making of those things that the English show their wisdom. But God is great! God is great! Here are stones which have been buried since the time of the holy Noah—peace be with him! I have lived on these lands for years. My father, and the father of my father, pitched their tents here before me; but they never heard of these figures. For twelve hundred years have the true believers been settled in this country, and none of them ever heard of a palace under ground."

Layard's smile grew broader as the Arab continued, "But lo! Here comes a Frank from many days' journey off, and he walks up to the very place, and he takes a stick, and makes a line here, and makes a line there. Here, says he, is the palace; there, says he, is the gate; and he shows us what has been all our lives beneath our feet, without our having known anything about it. Wonderful! Wonderful! Is it by books, is it by magic, is it by your prophets, that you have learned these things? Speak, O Bey! Tell me the secret of wisdom!"

Layard tried to explain. He delivered a brief speech on the advantages of civilization and of knowledge. The Sheikh still failed to grasp the importance of digging up old stones, nor could he imagine how Layard had found them so unerringly. The matter was dropped, and the wild, gay Arab festivities went on noisily to the dawn.

When the sun rose, the Arabs went, still singing and capering, to the mound. Hauling the bull along its trench was taxing but not complicated, and soon the great slab was at the edge of the plain. By removing the earth underneath it, Layard was able to slide his cart into place. The slab was ready to be dragged to the river.

Buffaloes were harnessed to the yoke, but the animals refused to budge when they felt the weight of the cart. It was necessary to haul it along by sheer manpower. A procession was formed: Layard riding first, to lead the way, followed by musicians, with their drums and fifes, "drumming and fifing with might and main." Then came the cart, "dragged by about three hundred men, all screeching at the top of their voices, and urged on by . . . the superintendents. The procession was closed by the women, who kept up the enthusiasm of the Arabs by their shrill cries." Abd-ur-Rahman's horsemen provided extra diversion by dashing backwards and forwards around the group, charging with their spears.

All went well until the cart came to the ruins of an abandoned Arab village nearby. In the local villages, pits were dug to store corn, barley and straw for the winter, and at the deserted village these pits had become filled with sand and dust, making them dangerous traps for the unwary.

Layard had carefully examined the plain before starting out, but one of these pits had escaped his notice. The cart bearing the bull passed over one, and two wheels sank in. "The Arabs pulled and yelled in vain," he writes. "The ropes broke, but the wheels refused to move. We tried every means to release them, but unsuccessfully. After working until dusk, we were obliged to give up the attempt."

Suspecting that roaming bands of desert Arabs might be attracted by the ropes, mats and felts, Layard left a party of his workmen to guard the cart. Sure enough, he was hardly in bed when the sound of war cries and gunshots reached him. He hurried to the scene and found that his men had beaten off an attack by the Jebour Arabs. The marauders had left their mark, unfortunately: a bullet had passed through the matting and had chipped away a bit of the stone. To this day, the scar can be seen on the great bull as it stands in the British Museum.

When morning came, the workmen placed thick planks under the wheels of the cart and got it out of the pit. The procession continued triumphantly on to within a few hundred yards of the river. This time, the cartwheels buried themselves in the sand, and it took most of the day to tug them free. The bull was finally transferred to the platform that was to hold it until the raft was ready. A tent was flung up around the platform, and another all-night celebration ensued.

It was back to the mound, now, to fetch the winged lion. To avoid a repeat of the cable-snapping episode, Layard bound the lion in double-thick cables, and it was low-ered safely. Two days later, lion and bull stood side by side on the banks of the Tigris, ready to head southward as soon as the rafts were ready.

When Layard had earlier sent sculptures down the river, they had gone by raft to Baghdad, where they were transferred to native-built boats that took them on to Basra. These boats were flimsy little things of poplar planks and reeds, and Layard knew they could never bear the weight of the lion or the bull.

He decided to try something revolutionary: to send the two big pieces all the way to Basra by raft. It was unheard-of to proceed past Baghdad with a raft. It was simply not done. Why? No one knew. It was not done, that was all. The raftmen of Mosul laughed when Layard ex-plained his plans.

"We do not go past Baghdad in rafts," they told him.

"Yes, but I want to try it!"

"We do not go past Baghdad in rafts," they replied inflexibly. They would not build him a raft, for they were certain it would be destroyed in the attempt to float past Baghdad.

Layard finally found a man at Baghdad who was willing to build rafts for him, though he, too, had doubts about Layard's sanity. Grumbling and muttering, he set to work, reluctantly building rafts according to Layard's spe-cial ideas, and shipping them in sections overland to Mosul.

The rafts were ready by April 20. The river had been low, which was unfavorable for navigation. But now there was a slight rise in the river. The two sculptures were ready. They had been placed on beams so that, by with-drawing wedges from under them, each would slide into the center of its raft.

That morning a long-faced Hormuzd Rassam came to Layard. "The men are on strike," he announced. "They want higher wages. There is a drought, and the crops are bad, and they need more money."

Some of the Arabs were already packing their tents to migrate to more fertile parts of the plain. Layard was faced with the loss of his workmen at a critical moment—with no choice but to increase their wages!

He let them go. Sheikh Abd-ur-Rahman's tribe was still nearby, and Layard asked them to help him. Another Arab tribe, camped some distance away, was also invited to join in the work. Finding they had been dismissed, the strikers suddenly backed down, only to find that Layard would not have their services at any price.

With his new helpers, Layard loaded the rafts, sending first the bull and then the lion sliding down the embankment, onto rafts supported by six hundred skins each. In a few hours both sculptures, and more than thirty cases of small objects, were safely strapped to the rafts. After another celebration, Layard gave two sheep to the raftmen to be slain on the bank of the river, as a sacrifice for the success of the trip. The meat was distributed among the poor, and the rafts began their slow journey down the river, with Layard's Baghdad raft-builder in charge, since Layard had more work to do at Mosul.

Layard wrote, "I watched the rafts until they disappeared behind a projecting bank forming a distant reach of the river. I could not forbear musing upon the strange destiny of their burdens; which, after adorning the palaces of the Assyrian kings, the objects of the wonder, and maybe the worship, of thousands, had been buried unknown for centuries beneath a soil trodden by Persians under Cyrus, by Greeks under Alexander, and by Arabs under the first descendants of their prophet. They were now to visit India, to cross the most distant seas of the southern hemisphere, and to be finally placed in a British Museum. Who can venture to foretell how their strange career will end?"

XI

It was now May 1847. Layard had been at work excavating since November 1845, with frequent interruptions. Most of this time he had concentrated on the mound of Nimroud. From time to time he had explored Kouyunjik, opposite Mosul. But he had never dug seriously there. He had poked and prodded the mound, scratched at its surface.

A little of his money still remained. He decided to use it up with one last dig at Kouyunjik. So, after carefully covering over the chambers at Nimroud with earth, to protect them from the elements, he closed his Nimroud headquarters, dismantled everything, and moved back to Mosul.

He had good reason to doubt that Kouyunjik held anything of value. Since it was right across the river from an important city, Layard thought that the natives had probably long since plundered the mound, removing the limestone slabs that once had been there—either using them whole as building-blocks, or burning them down for lime. Still, it was worth a try there, especially since the only other mound in the neighborhood, Nebbi Yunus, was a religious shrine and could not be touched.

With Kouyunjik so close to the town, Layard had a crowd of gaping onlookers to contend with every day. He rode to the mound in early morning, and toiled until dark.

His experiences at Nimroud had taught him what to expect in an Assyrian mound. He knew that the Assyrian kings had built their limestone palaces atop a platform of sun-dried bricks, thirty or forty feet high. The first step in digging for ruins, he wrote, "is to reach the platform of sun-dried bricks. When this is discovered, the trenches must be opened to the level of it, and not deeper; they should then be continued in opposite directions, care being always taken to keep along the platform." By trenching long enough, the excavator should eventually come to the walls of the palace.

At Kouyunjik, a twenty-foot layer of rubble and earth covered the ruins, and none of the diggers thus far, neither Botta nor Rouet nor Layard himself, had gotten down to the brick platform. Choosing the southwest corner of the mound, where he had been working in 1846, Layard determined to dig straight down until a platform emerged.

Several days of work turned up fragments of charred limestone, an encouraging sign. One morning, when Layard was in Mosul, two Arab women, their robes wet, came running to him with news:

"They have found sculptures in the mound!"

The women had hurried from the mound as soon as the first sculptures had emerged, and had swam across the Tigris to bring the news to Layard, since in the East the bearers of good tidings are entitled to a reward. Hardly had they received a few coins from the Englishman when Layard's overseer at Kouyunjik, a fat Nestorian named Toma Shishman, came huffing up.

"Sculptures!" the overseer panted. "Slabs—at Kouyunjik!"

"I know," Layard said with a grin, and pointed to the two Arab women. Fat Toma Shishman had come jogging across the bridge from Mosul, but the swimming girls had beaten him to the reward.

Another Assyrian palace! Layard was jubilant. He

immediately went to the mound, and found that his workmen had come across the walls and chambers of a fire-blackened palace very much like that at Nimroud. An entrance formed by winged bulls led to a second hall, with nine more chambers beyond.

"The palace," Layard wrote, "had been destroyed by fire. The alabaster slabs were almost reduced to lime, and many of them fell to pieces as soon as uncovered. The places which others had occupied could only be traced by a thin white deposit, left by the burnt alabaster upon the wall of sun-dried bricks, and having the appearance of a coating of plaster."

The chambers of the palace, as at Nimroud and Khorsabad, were long and narrow. The walls were of unbaked bricks, with a paneling of sculptured limestone slabs. The reliefs, though, were much larger than those at Nimroud, being ten feet high and eight to nine feet wide. The winged, human-headed bulls forming the entrances were fourteen to sixteen feet square!

Layard had no time for extensive digging now. He realized he had come upon a palace of great extent and magnificence, which must have been founded by one of the greatest of the Assyrian monarchs.

His labors in Assyria were now at a close, it seemed. His funds were exhausted and there was no reason to think that any more money would be available from the British Museum for a while. Layard wound up his affairs in Mosul, bid farewell to his workmen and his friends, paid a call on the current Pasha, and, on June 24, 1847, left Mosul, bound at last for England and accompanied by the faithful Hormuzd Rassam. It had been a fruitful two years. He had uncovered Assyrian palaces at two different mounds, had secured a vast array of treasures of art for his country, and had stirred a world-wide excitement and fascination over archaeology. As he left Mosul, the wives and daughters of his workmen clung to his horse, shedding tears and kissing his hand as he rode out of the city to begin his homeward journey.

Layard had never been one for rushing to his destination. Even though he had not set foot in England since 1839, he made his return journey in a wonderfully leisurely manner.

His first port of call was Constantinople, which he reached five weeks after leaving Mosul. Sir Stratford Canning was in England, and the Embassy was being run by one Lord Cowley, who welcomed Layard kindly and took him to see the Sultan again. He was introduced as "the man who had dug up the old stones."

Lord Cowley had some good news. Lord Aberdeen, Layard's enemy, had been replaced as Foreign Minister by Lord Palmerston, and Sir Stratford had wangled an appointment for Layard, making him at long last an official attaché of the British Embassy at Constantinople.

Oddly, this long-awaited news put Layard in an awkward position. He was in a hurry—of sorts—to get back to England, publish his findings, and display the drawings he was bringing back with him. But now, as a member of the Embassy at Constantinople, he needed formal permission to leave his post!

He wrote Sir Stratford for the needed permission, but "I received no answer to my application. He probably desired that, as he was about to return to Constantinople in order to complete the negotiations which were in process for the settlement of the Turco-Persian question, I should be on the spot to assist him."

Willy-nilly, Layard found himself stuck in Constantinople until Sir Stratford would allow him to go home. While he waited, he roamed the area, visiting a lake in Asia Minor, "attracted by the extreme beauty of the scenery, and unmindful of the malaria which notoriously prevailed in the locality."

The result was that he was soon down with his old ailment, and, shivering with fever, was taken back to Constantinople. The Embassy physician examined him and "insisted that I should leave the country without delay and return to England, or he would not answer for my life." Layard at once got permission to leave. At the end of October he embarked on board a French steamer for Malta.

Layard longed to revisit the scenes of his childhood. He took a steamer to Naples, went to Rome, where he showed his drawings of Nineveh to several Italian archaeologists, and then on to Florence to meet many old friends of his father and mother. His next stop was Paris.

Botta greeted him warmly there, and studied Layard's drawings. "Without any feeling of jealousy or rivalry he introduced me to his friends, and brought my discoveries, as much as possible, to the notice of the French public. I was introduced through him to the leading members of the French Institute, who gave me a special sitting in order that I might describe and explain to them the result of my explorations in the Assyrian ruins."

The meeting was opened by a venerable lawyer, toothless and nearly blind, who began to read a paper on the origin of Parliaments. Layard tells us that, "When, after an hour's preliminary discussion, he proceeded to divide his subject into five parts, with each of which the Academie was to be entertained in detail, the patience of that learned body became exhausted, and there was so strong a demonstration in favour of the opposition—the Nimroud antiquities—that the President was obliged to bring up the indignant lawyer in the middle of his course."

Layard advanced to the speaker's dais, and addressed the assembly in halting French. A question-and-answer session followed his speech. It rapidly turned into a shambles. The learned gentlemen of the Institute had so many questions to ask the discoverer of Nineveh that they stood on their chairs and shouted them out, and nothing could be heard through the confusion. Finally, quiet was restored, and it was proposed that Layard be given the honor of becoming a Corresponding Member of the Institute.

He left France a few days later, and arrived in England on December 22, 1847. He had been gone eight and a half years since leaving on what he then thought would be a one-year journey to Ceylon.

In 1839, setting out for the East, Layard had been a happy-go-lucky young man with no particular education, no visible means of support, and no position in the world. What a tremendous difference now!

He was a public figure. Not only was he a skilled diplomat attached to Her Majesty's Embassy in Constantinople, but he was the widely hailed "Nineveh" Layard, discoverer of the fabulous Assyrian palaces. He had met the Shah and the Sultan. He had been the confidante of a dozen tribal chiefs of the Near East, had engaged in delicate negotiations, had taken part in the most intimate workings of the British Embassy. Hardened by years of life in the Orient, he was fluent in Turkish and Arabic, able to withstand the rigors of any climate, a veteran traveler whose company was much in demand at social gatherings that winter.

Layard was the hero of the hour. Banquets and dinners galore celebrated his new fame. Oxford University awarded him an honorary degree. He sat for his portrait, and it became the frontispiece of one of his books. A contemporary writer describes the Layard of 1848 this way: "His face was singularly attractive and impressive. His figure suggested strength and power of endurance, rather than exceptional activity."

Exceptional activity was Layard's hallmark just now. He shifted from adventure to literature—and wrote the first best-seller in the history of archaeology.

XII

CONTROVERSY AND CUNEIFORM

Layard's schedule, here in 1848, was a hectic one. First, he wanted to write a popular book dealing with his exploits in Assyria. Secondly, he wished to arrange with the British Museum for the publication of the drawings of the monuments. Thirdly, he hoped to have Parliament vote him a sum of money large enough to allow him to return to Mosul and continue the excavations at Nimroud and Kouyunjik. Lastly, he was eager to examine the statuary he had shipped from Mosul, and to help arrange it for display in the British Museum.

These four goals met with varying degrees of success. Only the first, writing a book, worked out really well. Layard found a publisher, John Murray, who for many years had specialized in bringing out books on the Near East. Writing at what must have been a fantastic rate, Layard soon had finished a lengthy book which he called, in the long-winded manner of his day, *Nineveh and Its Remains, With an Account of a Visit to the Chaldean Christians of Kurdistan, and the Yezidis, or Devil-Worshippers; And an Inquiry into the Manners and Arts of the Ancient Assyrians.*

The book appeared in two thick volumes. Volume One and a third of Volume Two consisted of Layard's account of his travels and explorations from 1845 to 1847. He passed over his adventures from 1838 to 1845 in only a few pages, concentrating almost entirely on his life in Mosul. Describing in detail every step of his excavations, Layard also told of his many journeys into the surrounding regions, of his visits to the Nestorians, Kurds and Yezidis, along with lengthy descriptions of Arab life.

Layard put the same vigor and dash into his writing as into his life, and the result has been called "one of the best travel books ever written." The final two-thirds of the second volume was given over to an essay on the culture and arts of ancient Assyria as revealed by the excavations. This section—though it has largely been made obsolete by later discoveries—was erudite and scholarly, bristling with footnotes and learned references. Layard admitted that he received help from several members of the British Museum staff, notably Samuel Birch, the Keeper of Antiquities, in writing this section of his book.

In the book, Layard offered his opinions on the identity of the cities he had found. They were great cities, surely. But what cities were they?

He thought he knew. Tradition had long identified the mound of Kouyunjik with the site of Nineveh, and Layard was willing to accept that. But he believed that Kouyunjik was only *part* of Nineveh.

His evidence came from the Bible and from the Greek historians. The book of Jonah declares that "Nineveh was an exceeding great city of three days' journey." It tells how "Jonah began to enter into the city a day's journey," and states that Nineveh has "more than sixscore thousand persons that cannot discern between their right hand and their left hand."

The Greek Diodorus Siculus offered definite statistics on the size of Nineveh. Its dimensions, he wrote, were 150 stadia on each of the two longest sides, and 90 stadia each on the two shortest, making the circumference of the city walls 480 stadia, or 60 miles in modern measure.

Sixty miles? But the mounds opposite Mosul, Kouyunjik and Nebbi Yunus together, were only five miles in circumference!

Layard had an idea to account for this. Nimroud, he had decided, was the original Nineveh. Later kings expanded the city by building palaces at Kouyunjik and Khorsabad, and at the nearby mound of Karamles. This formed the expanded city—a sort of "Greater Nineveh"—that Diodorus Siculus had seen and Jonah had visited.

Indeed, this roughly fit Diodorus' measurements. Taking the four great mounds of Kouyunjik, Khorsabad, Karamles, and Nimroud as the corners of a square, the four sides corresponded pretty accurately to Diodorus' figure of 480 stadia or 60 miles, and with Jonah's statement that Nineveh was "an exceeding great city of three days' journey." The fact that there were no ruins to be found between the four great mounds was accounted for, Layard said, by the fact that the lesser houses, unlike the royal palaces, had been built of sun-dried bricks. These had long since crumbled away and disappeared.

Nineveh and Its Remains, when it appeared in 1849, was an immediate success, the smash best-seller of the season. It seemed as though everyone in England had to read the book, and it disappeared from the bookstalls as rapidly as John Murray could rush it into print. An American edition brought out in 1850 by George P. Putnam & Co. met with the same enthusiastic response. "Nineveh" was on everyone's lips.

Some of Layard's conclusions, though, came under immediate attack from scholars. The sharpest assault came from the historian George Rawlinson, the brother of Layard's friend and fellow-archaeologist, Henry Rawlinson.

George Rawlinson objected particularly to Layard's

idea that Nineveh had been sixty miles square and took in not only Kouyunjik but Nimroud, Khorsabad and Karamles as well. Rawlinson believed the traditional opinion: that Kouyunjik, and Kouyunjik alone, was the site of Nineveh.

He re-examined the Biblical evidence Layard had cited. Looking at the quote from Jonah, Rawlinson noted that "A city of three days' journey may be one which it requires three days to traverse from end to end, or one which is three days' journey in circumference, or, lastly one which can not be thoroughly visited and explored by a prophet commissioned to warn the inhabitants of a coming danger in less than three days' time." Rawlinson thought that the last idea was the correct one.

He turned also to Jonah's puzzling phrase, "six score thousand persons that cannot discern between their right hand and their left hand." If this meant "children," then Nineveh's population, including 120,000 children, would have been well over half a million, and could not have fit into the confines of Kouyunjik even under extreme crowding.

Rawlinson suggested that Jonah had meant that Nineveh's population was in a state of ignorance because it knew not God. Thus the "six score thousand persons that cannot discern between their right hand and their left hand" referred to the *entire* population—meaning Kouyunjik alone.

Until the cuneiform inscriptions of Assyria could be translated, there was no way of knowing who was right, Layard or George Rawlinson. For many years, scholars had been trying to crack the cuneiform code, but they had had little luck so far. So the dispute over the site of Nineveh remained up in the air for the time being.

Layard's book was a great success. But he did not do so well with his other aims. He had dreamed of publishing—helped by a British Museum subsidy—a large-size folio of drawings of the Assyrian monuments. The French government had published such a work for Botta—a magnificent five-volume set called *Monument de Ninive,* so named because Botta believed that Khorsabad was the site of Nineveh. Four of *Monument de Ninive*'s volumes contained steel-plate engravings of Flandin's marvelous drawings; the fifth volume was Botta's text.

Producing such a work was an enormously expensive proposition. The British Museum asked Parliament to vote £4000 for the task—$20,000. Despite the hubbub over Layard, Parliament refused.

Layard's publisher, John Murray, stepped into the breach and agreed to do a smaller series of illustrations engraved from Layard's drawings. It appeared late in 1849, and sold for the extremely high price of ten guineas—more than $50! It consisted of a large, flat portfolio containing dozens of excellent engravings of the Nimroud reliefs and winged bulls. Layard gave the collection the same title as Botta's book: *Monuments of Nineveh.*

The portfolio as issued did not contain any of Layard's copies of the inscriptions in cuneiform from Nimroud. He had wanted to publish these texts as working material for the scholars who were then trying to decipher Assyrian writing. Not until 1851, though, when the interest in Assyriology was at an even higher peak, did he finally get the inscriptions published, in a folio entitled *Inscriptions in the Cuneiform Character from Assyrian Monuments, discovered by A. H. Layard.*

Getting money from Parliament to resume the excavations posed problems also. In 1846, Sir Stratford Canning had arranged for a government grant of £2000 for Layard's work. The following year, another £500 was obtained, and then £800 more. So Layard's first expedition had cost Great Britain £3300, or something more than $15,000.

This was a small sum compared with what the French had spent on Botta. But to the British it seemed like a very great deal of money to be spending on old slabs of stone. The year 1848 was one of political uncertainty in Europe, with revolutions breaking out all over the continent, and Britain's Parliament was in a troubled, conservative mood. For a while it seemed as though no money at all would be voted to continue the excavations at Nimroud and Kouyunjik, despite the promising finds Layard had made in his last days at Mosul.

More unhappy news awaited Layard concerning the treasures he had shipped with such care from Nimroud. They had found their way, with many delays and change of ship, from Baghdad to Basra to Bombay, but there they had remained on the dock for many months while waiting for a suitable vessel to take them on to England. Not until April 1848 did fifty cases of Layard's antiquities finally leave Bombay aboard a newly built naval sailing ship. Some of the cases had been packed almost a year and a half before!

Nine days after the ship sailed, she ran into trouble at sea. A great storm struck her; her mast was knocked off, and for a while it seemed as if she would go down, taking with her the treasures of Nimroud. Finally the crippled vessel limped into port at Trincomalee, on Ceylon, where she had to undergo several months of repairs. It was only in October 1848 that the wandering packing cases made their long-overdue arrival in England.

Layard was present at the British Museum when the cases were opened. What he saw dismayed him beyond words. The larger sculptures had arrived in reasonably good shape, but the cases of small antiquities had suffered. They contained nothing but a jumble of fragments, so carelessly packed that they had been all but pulverized during the journey. The order in which Layard himself had placed the antiquities was disturbed, so that much information about the origin of the pieces was lost. Fragments of broken objects which Layard had painstakingly pieced together had been dispersed again. And some small objects of great artistic value had disappeared entirely!

An angry inquiry to Bombay produced the explanation. During the months that the cases had been sitting on the docks at Bombay, the British residents there had given way to the temptations of curiosity and had opened them to examine the Assyrian relics. There was even record of a certain clergyman having given an illustrated lecture on them! During the handling, a great deal of damage was done, and then the fragile antiquities were dumped back into their packing-cases in a careless and clumsy way.

The scandal that resulted shook up the administration of the Bombay docks, and from then on nobody tampered with British Museum property in Bombay. But that did not restore the broken wonders of Nimroud. Layard was plunged into despair by their fate.

In December 1848, with the manuscript of his book on the publisher's desk, Layard returned to Constantinople. He did not know whether he would ever dig at Nimroud and Kouyunjik again. But he was a member of the Embassy at Constantinople, and he felt that his place was at Sir Stratford Canning's side.

While Layard picked up the reins in Constantinople,

other men were trying to decipher the cuneiform inscriptions. The finds of Botta and Layard were terribly tantalizing. Nearly every slab was covered with cuneiform. But the cuneiform writing, looking very much like bird tracks made on sand, yielded no more meaning than real bird tracks would. It could not be read.

How frustrating that was! Long inscriptions, perhaps the annals of kings, poetry and history, texts of great length—all mute, all mysterious. If only there were some way of reading the inscriptions!

Long before Layard had ever seen the mounds of the Tigris, scholars were puzzling over cuneiform. Travelers had found cuneiform inscriptions not only in Mesopotamia but in Persia too, particularly at the ruins of the great Persian city of Persepolis. By 1778, the Persepolis inscriptions had been sorted into three groups. Class I was fairly simple, with only 42 different characters. But the Class II and Class III inscriptions were much more complex.

A German schoolmaster named Georg Friedrich Grotefend began to study the Persepolis inscriptions at the start of the nineteenth century. He knew that the problem of deciphering an unknown language was twofold. First, one had to assign correct sound values to the different characters. Then, these sounds had to be translated into meaningful words. For example, an American who sets out to learn Russian today must first find out what sounds the individual letters of the Russian alphabet stand for. Then, he must learn the meaning of those sounds. An American learning French only needs to master the second step, since French and English are written with the same sort of characters.

In 1802, Grotefend began with the Class I inscriptions of Persepolis. His theory was that in the early days of Persepolis, the Persians had written their language in cuneiform characters. Later on, they had shifted to an alphabetical system called Pehlevi, still speaking the same language but writing it in a different way. Now, Pehlevi was understood, and so was the Persian language. If Grotefend could match cuneiform signs to Persian words, it might be possible to go on to complete decipherment.

Over many years, he accomplished just that. By 1836, Old Persian, the Class I cuneiform, had been deciphered, thanks to Grotefend's extremely ingenious and laborious work.

There were two other kinds of cuneiform writing at Persepolis, though. One of them was the same kind that had been found on the inscriptions of Babylonia and Assyria. Was it possible to use Persian cuneiform as a key to deciphering Babylonian and Assyrian?

Several men tried. Foremost among them was a British lieutenant named Henry Creswicke Rawlinson (1810–1895). We have already seen him paying a visit to Layard at Mosul—and it was his brother George who had disagreed with Layard on the question of which mound was Nineveh.

At the age of 17, Henry Rawlinson had gone to India as a member of the First Bombay Grenadiers. Showing a great aptitude for languages, he soon had mastered not only several Indian tongues but Persian as well. Because of his linguistic abilities, Rawlinson was reassigned, in 1833, to Persia.

Rawlinson was, naturally, interested in the ancient languages of Persia. In the spring of 1835, he paid a visit to the Behistun Rock near Kermanshah, which Layard had seen a few years later. The Rock was an impressive sight, rising perpendicularly to a height of 1700 feet. On a prepared surface, 60 by 23 feet, more than 300 feet above the ground, a sculptured bas-relief and a cuneiform inscription had been carved.

No one understood what this inscription and bas-relief represented. We now know that the Persian king Darius had had it carved to celebrate his triumph over a rebellion in his land, but when Rawlinson visited the Behistun Rock the relief had been identified by at least one traveler as "representatives of the Ten Tribes of Israel standing before a King of Assyria and the Medes."

Rawlinson was aware of Grotefend's work, but did not have a copy of the German's decipherments. So Rawlinson had to do all of Grotefend's work over again. He quickly discovered that the Behistun inscription was in three different cuneiform types—the familiar Class I, which Grotefend had identified as Old Persian; Class II, which had been identified as a language called Elamite or Susian; and Class III, the writing of Babylonia and Assyria.

Rawlinson's first step was to make copies of the inscriptions. This was no simple job, since the rock was all but impossible to climb. In the summer and autumn of 1835, he began to copy the 414 lines of the Class I text by climbing down to the rock ledge of the carvings from above, on ladders and ropes. By late 1837, working on and off, he had managed to copy only about 200 lines, and had deciphered and translated the first two paragraphs.

Rawlinson's military duties kept him away from Behistun for some years afterward. In the summer of 1843, he was named to succeed Colonel Taylor as the East India Company's Resident in Baghdad. Arriving in December 1843, he examined the nearby ruins of Babylon, and had some correspondence with Layard, who was then in Constantinople.

In the summer of 1844, Rawlinson made the thousand-mile journey from Baghdad to Behistun and copied the complete Class I, or Old Persian, inscription, and the total 263 lines of the Class II, or Elamite, inscription adjoining it. The Class III, or Babylonian, inscription was beyond his reach in an inaccessible part of the cliff.

Rawlinson now was able to translate the whole Class I inscription with confidence. He began to approach the more difficult Class II, or Elamite.

Meanwhile, first Botta and then Layard announced their spectacular finds near Mosul. With the wealth of new Assyrian inscriptions emerging, it suddenly became important to be able to translate the writing of Mesopotamia. Rawlinson returned to Behistun to make a copy of the Class III, or Babylonian, inscription.

At first glance it seemed impossible to reach the inscription. Rawlinson, like Layard, had little respect for the word "impossible." He found "a wild Kurdish boy, who had come from a distance," who scrambled up the rock and made paper "squeezes" of the inscription.

The decipherment of Babylonian-Assyrian cuneiform was an inch-by-inch proposition. A letter at a time had to be puzzled out. Rawlinson was not alone in attacking the job. An Irish scholar named Hincks added much that was of value, as did the German-French Jules Oppert and the British W. H. Fox Talbot. There were often disagreements among these four, and their early readings of the texts sometimes were widely different. We find Hincks translating one royal name—Sennacherib's—as *Sin-ki-ram*, while Rawlinson reads the same name as *Bel-adonim-sa!* Sometimes they were closer, as when Hincks read a name as *Divanurish* and Rawlinson as *Divanukha* (They were both wrong on that one, as it turned out!).

It was a slow, fumbling procedure, with many mistakes along the way. The wonder of it, though, is not that they made mistakes but that they succeeded at all. By 1851, Rawlinson published his great work, *Memoir on the Babylonian and Assyrian Inscriptions*, and after that it was simply a matter of refining and polishing the understanding of the cuneiform texts. The basic job had been done.

It had all happened quite quickly—so very quickly that Layard in 1853 wrote in wonder, "When in 1849 I published the narrative of my first researches in Assyria, the numerous inscriptions recovered from the remains of the buried palaces were still almost a sealed book. . . . I then, however, expressed my belief, that ere long their contents would be known with almost certainty, and that they would be found to furnish a history, previously almost unknown, of one of the earliest and most powerful empires of the ancient world. Since that time the labors of English scholars, and especially of Col. Rawlinson and Dr. Hincks, and of . . . other eminent investigators on the Continent, have nearly led to the fulfillment of those anticipations."

The cuneiform code had been cracked. And Layard, who was off in Assyria while most of the work was being done, soon came back to England, bringing a fresh load of inscriptions to keep the scholars busy.

XIII

THE PALACES OF NINEVEH

While Rawlinson and Hincks toiled over the cuneiform inscriptions, Layard was in Constantinople, working
at the British Embassy. He received no pay at first, and that
led him to be sarcastic many years later in his book *Early
Adventures*, when he referred to "his return at the end of
the same year [1848] to Constantinople, where I had been
appointed, as a reward for my various services, an unpaid
attaché to Her Majesty's Embassy."

While in Constantinople, Layard learned for the first
time what a great success his book was having back in
England. He was delighted, of course. The royalties earned
would be considerable and would help him recover from the
financial strain of his excavations. He wrote to his old
traveling companion, Mitford (who had actually reached
Ceylon and was living there): "Of notoriety I have plenty,
and the very liberal arrangement of my publishers has en-
abled me to realize a *very handsome* sum. Nearly 8000
copies were sold in the year—a new edition is in the press,
and Murray anticipates a continual steady demand for the
book, which will place it side by side with Mrs. Rundell's
Cookery." It was soon necessary to bring out an abridged
one-volume edition to meet the heavy demand.

Layard's unpaid status at the Embassy soon ended. In
April 1849, Lord Palmerston promoted him to a paid post.
At the same time, the British Museum requested that Lay-
ard be released from his diplomatic duties and sent to
Mosul to resume his archaeological career.

Parliament voted an appropriation to cover the costs of the work. The British Museum asked for £4000 on Layard's behalf, but only £3000 was forthcoming, this to be spread out over two years of excavation.

Layard's loyalty to Sir Stratford Canning kept him at Constantinople until August 28, 1849, performing routine Embassy duties that he was better equipped to handle than anyone else. Finally he began to return to Mosul. This time the expedition was a well-equipped one. Layard was accompanied not only by Hormuzd Rassam, who was to assist him at the excavations, but by a young English artist named Cooper, who had the assignment of making sketches of everything that was discovered. The expedition also had its own physician, an English doctor named Sandwith.

Typically, Layard took a new route from Constantinople to Mosul. He traveled by way of Armenia and Kurdistan, moving at his usual leisurely pace, stopping off here and there to investigate interesting tribes or unusual ruins.

Soon, the party drew near Mosul. In an outlying village, Layard met many of his old workmen and superintendents, and they greeted him joyfully. Fat old Toma Shishman was there, glad to hear that Layard would be digging again. The travelers proceeded on to Mosul.

Layard hastened over the creaking bridge of boats and jostled his way through the crowded bazaars, pausing now and then to glance at the long line of lofty mounds just across the river, with the vast bulk of Kouyunjik dominating everything. He came to the house he had left two years before, and old servants moved into their familiar places. "Indeed," he wrote, "it seemed as if we had but returned from a summer's ride. Two years had passed away like a dream."

Layard's second expedition had a purpose somewhat different from that of the first. In 1845-1847, his chief interest had been finding sculpture and other works of art. Now the halls of the British Museum were well stocked with Assyrian palace reliefs, and the sudden breakthrough in cuneiform decipherment made it more important to find new cuneiform texts. So it was for inscriptions this time, rather than reliefs, that Layard had come to search.

On the morning after his arrival, he rode across to Kouyunjik where his friend Ross, a member of the English colony at Mosul, had carried on small-scale work since Layard's departure in June 1847. After Ross' own departure the following year, the English Vice-Consul, Christian Rassam, had continued the work.

The mound looked much as it had when Layard left it. A few new chambers had been cleared, and more sculptured reliefs had been found, showing the conquest by an Assyrian king of a river-dwelling nation. In the process of clearing these chambers, the rubbish-heap near the palace site had grown to a height of more than thirty feet. The workmen, under Toma Shishman's supervision, had cut tunnels through the mound, propping up their sides with wooden beams and columns of earth, as in mines. Layard wrote, "These long galleries, dimly lighted, lined with the remains of ancient art, broken urns projecting from the crumbling sides, and the wild Arab and hardy Nestorian wandering through their intricacies, or working in their dark recesses, were singularly picturesque."

Layard now prepared to take over the direction of the work once again. He reassembled his old team of workmen and supervisors. As word spread of his return, many of his Nestorian diggers came down to Mosul from their mountain homes, and he hired Jebour Arabs from the neighborhood to aid them. Under the new working methods, the diggers would toil in the subterranean galleries, and baskets on pulleys would carry the removed earth to the surface.

Before he could begin, Layard felt it necessary to call on the governor. Some six or seven pashas had come and gone in Layard's absence, and the current office-holder was Kiamil Pasha, who had previously been Turkish Ambassador to Berlin, and whom Layard describes as having "eminently courteous and polished manners. His intelligence, and what is of far more importance in a Turkish governor, his integrity, were acknowledged." Layard contrasted him favorably with the one-eyed ogre, Mohammed Pasha, who had ruled Mosul at Layard's first arrival in 1845. Somewhat to Layard's surprise, Mohammed Pasha —though condemned to death for his misdeeds at Mosul —had bribed his way to power again and was, in 1849, ruling a district in Asia Minor!

By October 12, Layard had work under way at Kouyunjik, with 100 workmen divided into a dozen gangs. With things going smoothly enough there, Layard and Hormuzd Rassam rode down to inspect Nimroud on October 18, reaching it the following morning.

"By sunrise," Layard writes, "I was amongst the ruins. The mound had undergone no change. There it rose from the plain, the same sun-burnt yellow heap that it had stood for twenty centuries. The earth and rubbish, which had been heaped over the excavated chambers and sculptured slabs, had settled, and had left uncovered in sinking the upper part of several bas-reliefs. A few colossal heads of winged figures rose calmly above the level of the soil, and with two pairs of winged bulls, which had not been reburied on account of their mutilated condition, was all that remained above ground of the Northwest Palace, that great storehouse of the Assyrian history and art. Since my departure the surface of the mound had again been furrowed by the plough, and ample crops had this year rewarded the labors of the husbandman. The ruins of the Southwest Palace were still uncovered. The Arabs had respected the few bas-reliefs which stood against the crumbling walls, and Saleh Shahir pointed to them as a proof of the watchfulness of his people during my long absence."

Layard called together some of his old workmen, and set them to digging at the still largely unexplored Northwest Palace, and at a center palace which had not been explored at all. Layard also had a tunnel made on the site of a high conical mound at the northwest corner of Nimroud. On his earlier expedition, Layard had dug a forty-foot shaft through this mound, which he referred to as "the pyramid," but had found nothing in it but sun-dried bricks.

Botta had found a similar brick structure at Khorsabad, and had called it an "observatory." A few decades later, such brick towers would be discovered at every Assyrian, Babylonian and Sumerian city, and their rightful purpose understood. These towers were called *ziggurats* by the ancients. Rising in a series of set-back stages, they were topped by temples, and served as the religious focal point of each town. The *ziggurats* at Khorsabad and Nimroud were small ones, but in the southern cities they were imposing structures, so great in size that one, the *ziggurat* of Babylon, passed into the Old Testament as the Tower of Babel, whose impious builders had tried to reach the vault of Heaven itself.

On the second day of Layard's stay at Nimroud, he awoke to find that travelers had arrived during the night. Descending into the mound, Layard found, "beneath, in an excavated chamber, wrapped in his travelling cloak, Rawlinson, deep in sleep, wearied by a long and harassing night's ride." Henry Rawlinson was on his way back to England to work on his translation of the Behistun inscription, and he had stopped off to see his old friend Layard. They had much to talk about. They had become close friends on earlier meetings, because they had so much in common— a love of adventure as well as of antiquity. Rawlinson, every bit as dashing as Layard, had once made himself famous by riding 750 miles in 150 consecutive hours to warn the British Ambassador at Teheran of the arrival in Persia of a notorious Russian spy. That was the sort of exploit that could endear a man to Henry Layard for life.

For two days Rawlinson rested, overcome by fatigue and fever, at Nimroud, and on the third day Layard took him up to Kouyunjik to view the palace of Sennacherib. "After a hasty survey of the ruins," Layard tells us, "we parted, and he continued his journey to Constantinople and to England, to reap the laurels of a well-earned fame."

During October and November, Layard divided his time between Nimroud and Kouyunjik, carrying on excavations at both mounds at the same time. Cooper, the artist, remained at Mosul to sketch the Kouyunjik palace reliefs, but he was troubled by ill health and accomplished less than a healthy man might have done. Hormuzd Rassam served as Layard's right hand, toiling tirelessly to superintend the operations.

The Kouyunjik workmen received their pay in the subterranean galleries, those of Nimroud in their village. "A scene of wild confusion ensued on these occasions," Layard writes. The workmen would scream and gesticulate when they felt they were being underpaid, but Rassam somehow contrived to keep order. When the Arabs at Kouyunjik had been paid, Layard notes, they would cross the river to Mosul and "walk through the town in martial array, brandishing their weapons and chanting their war cries in chorus, to the alarm of the authorities and the inhabitants, who generally concluded that the place had been invaded by the Bedouins. It was Mr. Hormuzd Rassam's task to keep in check these wild spirits."

Among the new finds at Nimroud was a sculptured slab depicting a subject Layard knew all about: transporting the giant winged bulls. The ancient reliefs showed every step in the process as it had been handled 2500 years earlier.

The technique was not much different from the one Layard had used. The bull had been placed on a thick wooden sledge, dragged by four cables pulled by small ropes wound around the shoulders of workmen. The sledge moved over rollers, which, as soon as left behind by the sledge, were picked up and carried around in front of it again. The bull was lowered into place with an arrangement of wooden props and cables, just as Layard had removed it thousands of years afterward.

"On the bull itself," Layard wrote, "are four persons, probably the superintending officers. The first is kneeling, and appears to be clapping his hands, probably beating time, to regulate the motions of the workmen, who unless they applied their strength at one and the same moment would be unable to move so large a weight. Behind him stands a second officer with outstretched arm, evidently giving the word of command. The next holds to his mouth, either a speaking-trumpet, or an instrument of music. . . . The fourth officer, also standing, carries a mace, and is probably stationed behind to give directions to those who work the levers. The sledge bearing the sculpture is followed by men with coils of ropes and various implements, and drawing carts laden with cables and beams. Even the landscape is not neglected; and the country in which these operations took place is indicated by trees, and by a river. In this stream are seen men swimming on skins; and boats and rafts, resembling those still in use in Assyria, are impelled by oars with wedge-shaped blades."

Thanks to the work of Rawlinson, Hincks, and others, it was now possible to make tentative translations of the inscriptions at Nimroud and Kouyunjik. At long last, Layard learned who had built his rediscovered cities, and what cities they had been. Until now he had worked in the dark. Suddenly came a blaze of light.

Kouyunjik was shown to have been Nineveh. That settled the argument Layard had had with George Rawlinson, and Rawlinson was right. There had never been any vast Assyrian city sprawling over 216 square miles, as Layard had claimed. Each mound had been a different city, and Kouyunjik had been Nineveh.

The mound at Khorsabad, where Botta had dug, was identified as the Assyrian city of Dur-Sharrukin, built by King Sargon II, who had ruled from 721 to 705 B.C. So Botta, too, had been wrong in thinking that Khorsabad was part of Nineveh.

The mound of Nimroud, Layard now learned, had been the city of Calah, or Kalhu. The Bible and the Arab legends had credited the legendary Nimrod with founding Calah. But the cuneiform inscriptions revealed that it had been built by the Assyrian King Shalmaneser I, who ruled from 1280 to 1261 B.C. As for Karamles, the fourth corner of Layard's gigantic imagined Nineveh, it turned out to be an unimportant provincial town built by Sargon II, the Khorsabad king.

The kings who had built Layard's palaces at Nimroud and Kouyunjik were revealed now too. The Kouyunjik palace was shown by Dr. Hincks to be the work of Sennacherib, the insane, ferocious monarch who ruled Assyria between 704 and 681 B.C. One of the Nimroud palaces, it developed, had been built by Sennacherib's son and successor, Esarhaddon. During his reign, which lasted from 680 to 669 B.C., Esarhaddon had rebuilt Babylon, which his mad father had destroyed in a vengeful rage. Esarhaddon had also made the ancient land of Egypt an Assyrian province for a brief time.

A second Nimroud palace (the "Northwest Palace") also bore Esarhaddon's name. But it shortly became clear that he had not built this one; he had simply inhabited it for a while and had had his own name inscribed on its walls. Dr. Hincks read the name of the true builder as Ashurakhbal. After a while, it developed that the reading was incorrect; the name was actually Assurnasirpal, a great Assyrian conqueror who had held the throne from 885 to 859 B.C., two centuries before Esarhaddon. Assurnasirpal was the king shown in the wonderful lion-hunt relief Layard had found at Nimroud. The sort of person Assurnasirpal was is chillingly made clear by this inscription, which Layard found on the walls of the Northwest Palace at Nimroud and which was first translated about 1870:

"Their men, young and old, I, Assurnasirpal, took prisoners. Of some I cut off the feet and hands; of others I cut off the noses, ears, and lips; of the young men's ears I made a heap; of the old men's heads I built a tower. I exposed their heads as a trophy in front of their city. The male children and the female children I burned in the flames."

At Kouyunjik, Layard uncovered another entrance to

Sennacherib's palace. Two colossal winged bulls framed the entrance, which was nearly fifteen feet wide. The sculptures were buried in a mass of brick and earth, mingled with charcoal and charred wood, telling a grim tale of the sack of Nineveh by the invading Medes. The marks of chariot wheels could still be seen in the pathway between the bulls.

"It would be difficult to describe the effect produced, or the reflections suggested by these solemn and majestic figures, dimly visible amidst the gloom, when, after winding through the dark, underground passages, you suddenly came into their presence," Layard wrote. "Between them Sennacherib and his hosts had gone forth in all their might and glory to the conquest of distant lands, and had returned rich with spoil and captives, amongst whom may have been the handmaidens and wealth of Israel. Through them, too, the Assyrian monarch had entered his capital in shame, after his last and fatal defeat. Then the lofty walls, now but long lines of low, wave-like mounds, had stretched far to the right and to the left—a basement of stone supporting a curtain of solid brick masonry, crowned with battlements and studded with frowning towers."

At Nimroud, meanwhile, the workman had been clearing the brick tower that Layard called "the pyramid." He saw now that it was not a pyramid at all, but rather a square tower rising in set-back stages. Before its ruin, it must have been almost 200 feet high. Layard did not, of course, have any idea of the role of the *ziggurat* as a temple-tower in Mesopotamia, and he guessed that the tower was a tomb: the tomb of Sardanapalus (the Greek name for Assurbanipal), one of the last Assyrian kings. Every pioneer is entitled to a few wrong guesses, and this was part of Layard's quota.

Early in December, at Kouyunjik, Layard found more bulls, most of them damaged as though by an earthquake. A vast hall, 180 feet long, was lined with these limestone colossi, a dozen in all.

One of the important features of this promenade of bulls was the existence of a continuous inscription, 152 lines long, carried across four pairs of bulls. Layard carefully copied this and forwarded it to Henry Rawlinson in England, and after prolonged study Rawlinson revealed that the inscription was nothing less than Sennacherib's annals of six years of warfare. This grisly record of conquest and looting confirmed the Biblical accounts in many places, showing that the Old Testament was at least in part an accurate historical document.

"Hezekiah, king of Judah," Sennacherib declared, "who had not submitted to my authority, forty-six of his principal cities, and fortresses and villages depending upon them, of which I took no account, I captured and carried away their spoil. I shut up Hezekiah himself within Jerusalem, his capital city. The fortified towns, and the rest of his towns, which I spoiled, I served from his country, and gave to the kings of Ascalon, Ekron, and Gaza, so as to make his country small. In addition to the former tribute imposed upon their countries, I added a tribute, the nature of which I fixed."

The rest of the passage had been defaced and could not be translated. But the story can be found in II Kings, chapter 18:

"Now in the fourteenth year of King Hezekiah did Sennacherib king of Assyria come up against all the fenced cities of Judah, and took them. And Hezekiah king of Judah sent to the king of Assyria to Lachish, saying, I have offended; return from me: that which thou puttest on me will I bear. And the king of Assyria appointed unto Hezekiah king of Judah [a tribute of] three hundred talents of silver and thirty talents of gold."

After quoting a number of Sennacherib's statements, Layard writes—and surely he can be forgiven the note of pride in his words—"Little doubt, I trust, can now exist in the minds of my readers as to the identification of the builder of the palace of Kouyunjik with the Sennacherib of scripture."

Layard spent most of December at Nimroud. During his first visit, he had buried for safekeeping several gigantic human-headed winged lions, and now they were dug up and transported to the river for shipment to England. This task took three months, since, as before, a twenty-foot-deep trench had to be dug in order to get the colossi down from the mound to the plain.

Layard's work was rendered more lively in mid-December by an Arab attack. He woke one morning to hear the sound of shouting and gunfire, and, leaving his house, found a scene of wild excitement and confusion. Horsemen, "galloping in all directions and singing their war song, were driving before them with their long spears the cattle and sheep of the inhabitants of the village. The men were firing at the invaders; the women, armed with tent poles and pitchforks, and filling the air with their shrill screams, were trying to rescue the animals."

Layard rapidly discovered what was taking place. The marauding Arabs of the Tai tribe had come into the village under cover of heavy fog to loot the townsfolk. It seemed that some days before, the Jebour Arabs—the tribe from which Layard had drawn most of his workmen—had stolen some camels from the Tai. Now the Tai had come to even the score.

The situation promised to get rapidly out of hand. Already, some of Layard's Jebours had mounted the conical mound he called "The Tomb of Sardanapalus," and were collecting stones and bricks to hurl down at the Tai. Others, brandishing swords and spears, were ready to do battle with the invaders.

Sending Hormuzd Rassam to keep the Jebours calm, Layard sought the Tai chief, Saleh, and tried to negotiate. With his astonishing skill as a peacemaker, Layard was able to halt the quarrel in a few minutes. The Tai sheikh agreed to return all that his men had taken, and Layard promised that he would compel the Jebours to give up the stolen camels. Sheikh Saleh retreated peacefully after Layard promised to honor the Tai encampment with a visit in the next few days.

Two days later, he set out for the Tai tents, on the far side of the River Zab. Recent rains, however, had swollen the river, and it was impossible to ford it. Spending Christmas day at Nimroud, Layard tried again on December 28. They found a place where they could cross the river this time. As they approached the Arab camp, some women and children came out to peer at the strangers, and one woman cried, "Look, look! This is the one who is come from the other end of the world to dig up the bones of our grandfathers and grandmothers!"

It was spoken in resentful tones. But the sheikhs of the Tai welcomed Layard gladly, and a feast commenced that lasted far into the night.

By January 28, 1850, Layard was ready to haul the colossal winged lions out of the Northwest Palace of Nimroud and down to the river for shipment to Baghdad. On a calm cloudless night, he and Rassam rode out to take one last look at the huge works before they left their old resting-places.

"The moon was at her full," Layard tells us, "and as we drew nigh to the edge of the deep wall of earth rising around them, her soft light was creeping over the stern features of the human heads, and driving before it the dark shadows which still clothed the lion forms. One by one the limbs of the giant sphinxes emerged from the gloom, until the monsters were unveiled before us. I shall never forget that night, or the emotions which those venerable figures caused within me. A few hours more and they were to stand no longer where they had stood unscathed amidst the wreck of man and his works for ages."

Before they could depart their ancient sites, though, six days of work were needed, three for each lion. Recent heavy rains had turned the plain of Nimroud to a swamp, and it was no easy matter to haul the carts bearing the lions to the river. Again and again, the wheels of the carts became mired in muck. Layard's artist, Cooper, was present to sketch the moving, but the Arabs decided that he had the "evil eye," and was bringing bad luck. The luckless Cooper had to withdraw. A few yards later, the cart bogged down again. This time, one of the Arabs was picked as the bearer of the "evil eye," and was banished from the site. On and on the cart crawled, the superstitious Arabs finding a hundred reasons for the slow progress, until at the end the exasperated Layard seized one of the ropes himself and helped to haul the carts along.

The lions stood at the river's edge for a few days while the rafts were made ready. The river was then at low ebb, but it unexpectedly rose to torrential levels. The plain of

Nimroud became "one vast sea, and a furious wind drove the waves against the foot of the mound. The Arabs had never seen a similar inundation, and before they could escape to the high lands many persons were overwhelmed in the waters."

When the flood subsided, Layard anxiously went looking for his lions. There they stood, covered with mud and silt, but unharmed. Unhappily, one of the lions broke in half while being loaded on its raft, and a stranger maliciously broke the nose of the other during the night.

The adventures of the lions were not yet over. They reached Baghdad safely, the rafts were repaired and reinflated, and off went the lions to Basra. En route, an embankment burst and one raft was swept off into the middle of a swamp a mile away. The other lion reached Basra safely. Some time later, an English steamer penetrated into the swamp and found the stranded lion—the broken one, as it happened. Both lions eventually made their way to London, and the damage they had suffered was repaired by British Museum experts.

In February, Layard tried to return to Qalah Shergat, the mound where he had found the black basalt statue of Shalmaneser III, and so little else, on his first expedition. But the mound was surrounded by an unruly tribe of Arabs. Layard alone would not have hesitated to venture into their midst, but he could not safely bring his whole staff of superintendents and workmen into such a dangerous area, so he abandoned the idea.

After a lengthy tour of the area west of Mosul—which turned up some interesting mounds that Layard had no time to explore, along the Khabar River—he returned to Kouyunjik. One of the biggest discoveries of his career was waiting there for him.

XIV

In Layard's absence, Toma Shishman had continued to clear away the rubble covering Sennacherib's palace at Nineveh. New chambers had appeared, walled in by the usual sculptured limestone slabs. At the western side of these chambers, the slabs were curved backward, showing the enormous pressure they had been under when the upper part of the building had caved in upon them.

Layard inspected the newly discovered chambers. A large doorway, guarded by carved representations of the fish-god Dagon, led to two smaller chambers whose floors were covered, to a depth of more than a foot, with clay tablets bearing cuneiform inscriptions!

On his first expedition, Layard had come across some similar clay tablets and had not fully understood what they were. In some of them, the cuneiform writing was so minute it could be read only under a magnifying glass; to the naked eye it seemed to be just a form of decoration. Unaware of their true significance, Layard had not packed the tablets with any great care, and most of them had been ground to powder on their roundabout journey to London.

This time, Layard knew well enough that he had stumbled over something of major importance. The tablets were of different sizes, some of them flat and as large as 6½ by 9 inches, others convex, no more than an inch long, and covered with microscopic writing. The chambers held nothing less than the official state archives of Assyria in Sennacherib's time. A few years earlier, the tablets would have been just so many tantalizing lumps of clay—but now, with scholars able to decipher cuneiform, the library of Sennacherib promised to tell a vivid story, and it was a promise that was kept.

Layard's new discovery brought Assyria to life. Here, set down by ancient unknown scribes, were the records of grim wars and distant expeditions undertaken by Assyrian armies. Here were royal decrees, straight from the lips of the mad Sennacherib. Here were lists of the names of the gods, and registers of the offerings in the temples—so many jars of grain, so much wine, so many goats. One tablet bore a list of the sacred days of each month. Another was an Assyrian calendar.

An entire culture was revealed—both the bloody harshness of Assyrian warfare and the gentler details of daily life. In one grand swoop, the number of available Assyrian texts was multiplied a hundredfold. Probably the most significant of the tablets from Sennacherib's library was the one on which Dr. Hincks, in Layard's words, "detected a table of the value of certain cuneiform letters, expressed by different alphabetical signs." This, and many like it found afterward, were dictionaries! They were invaluable in solving the many puzzles that still remained in the decipherment of Assyrian writing.

The dictionary tablets also stirred up a new puzzle of their own. In parallel columns, they provided lists of Assyrian words and their equivalents in an unknown language resembling no other tongue. It was many years before this mystifying language was identified as that of the Sumerians, the race that had inhabited Mesopotamia before the arrival of the Semitic-speaking invaders around 2400 B.C. The tablets were Assyrian-Sumerian dictionaries, written by scribes for the benefit of the priests, who needed to understand the ancient Sumerian language since it was still used in Assyrian religious rituals. Without the dictionaries from Nineveh, it is doubtful that Sumerian would ever have been deciphered.

The scholars of Europe were given even more work to do a few years later, after Layard's departure from Mosul. Hormuzd Rassam, digging in the palace of Assurbanipal at Kouyunjik, came upon yet another horde of tablets. Assurbanipal, Sennacherib's grandson, had caused all the literature of Mesopotamia to be transcribed on new tablets and stored at his palace. Since Mesopotamian literature was more than 2000 years old even in his day, the treasure-trove was a fabulous one. Layard's find and Rassam's together totaled no less than 26,000 tablets! Some of these, naturally, were broken fragments, but even allowing for "joins" the total ran well over 20,000.

As soon as this vast library reached Europe, the foremost Assyriologists of the day began to attack it and translate it. They found that the texts could be divided into five general categories: historical literature, the private library of the king, the library of the temple, correspondence, and business contracts. Not only did a wealth of mythological material appear, but information about Assyrian politics and government, commerce, religious practice—the whole life of a people.

Naturally, it took many years before the tablets were fully examined, let alone translated. One of the most amazing stories concerning Sennacherib's library occurred long after Layard had retired from archaeology, but deserves to be mentioned at this point.

It began in 1872, at the British Museum. A young philologist named George Smith had been working at the museum since 1866, helping to sort through the enormous collection of tablets that Layard had found at Kouyunjik. Smith was a protégé of Henry Rawlinson, who was now devoting all his time to the study of cuneiform texts. In 1872, Smith was sorting through the fragments of the tablets from Sennacherib's library when he came upon a startling one: part of an inscription that told the legend of a great flood, very much like the Biblical deluge of Noah! Smith hastily began to search through the rest of the fragments to find more of the story. He recognized the great importance of uncovering an Assyrian myth that paralleled the Biblical account.

When Smith published his story, the public excitement was as great as it had been when Layard first found Nineveh, a generation before. Smith let it be known that he believed the remainder of the Deluge story could be unearthed at Kouyunjik, and a British newspaper, the *Daily Telegraph*, came forward to advance him the sum of a thousand guineas (more than $5000) to go to Mosul and search Kouyunjik for the rest of the text.

Smith received a six-month leave from the British Museum, and left immediately for the near East, in January 1873. It was a strange quest. He was a philologist, not an archaeologist and he had no experience in excavation. Nor had he ever traveled before. So much of a greenhorn was Smith that he so arranged things as to arrive at Mosul during the hot season—when even Layard, indomitable as he was, had been forced to abandon work.

Stranger still was the needle-in-a-haystack aspect of his search. Smith proposed to enter a vast mound, rummage around in the rubbish, and find precisely the fragments he was looking for to complete the Deluge story! It seemed like a wild idea.

He arrived in Mosul in May, hired some men, had

the customary quarrels with the governor, and began digging in the part of Sennacherib's palace that Layard had referred to as the "chambers of record." Dozens of tablets turned up, scattered in the dirt. Smith found three thousand tablets in all, and made the discovery that the library had originally been in an upper story of the palace, but had fallen through to a lower floor when the palace was sacked.

Then came the miracle. On the fifth day of work, he writes, "I sat down to examine the store of fragments of cuneiform inscriptions from the day's digging, taking out and brushing off the earth from the fragments to read their contents. On cleaning one of them I found to my surprise and gratification that it contained the greater portion of the seventeen lines of inscription belonging to the first column of the Chaldean [Mesopotamian] account of the Deluge, and fitting into the only place where there was a serious blank in the story."

Smith sent news of his jackpot find back to the *Daily Telegraph*, and touched off a nine days' wonder in England at the improbable success of his mission. To reach into a mound of rubble and come up with exactly the right fragment—how unlikely it seemed!

Today nearly the complete Deluge story exists in a number of versions, and we know that what Layard found and Smith translated was an Assyrian translation of an extremely ancient Sumerian poem. The hero of the story is Utnapishtim, the Assyrian Noah, whose tale is told as part of the epic of another ancient hero, Gilgamesh—the Mesopotamian equivalent of Hercules and Odysseus combined —whose name Smith faultily translated as "Izdubar." The Deluge story as told in the Nineveh tablets is strikingly like that of the Bible in many ways. Utnapishtim declares:

"All that I possessed of the seed of life I gathered together, the whole I made to enter into the ship; all my servants, male and female, the tame animals of the fields, and the wild animals of the plains, and the young men of the army, all these I made to enter. And Shamash [the sun-god] caused a great flood, and he spake, speaking in the darkness of the night: 'I will cause it to rain from the heavens abundantly; enter within the ship and close its door.'

"I entered into the ship and shut its door. . . . The fury of the tempest arose in the morning. Destruction marched over the mountains and the plains. . . . The waters destroyed all life from the face of the earth. Six days and six nights passed: the thunder, the storm, and the winds reigned. In the middle of the seventh day the tempest ceased. . . . I was borne over the sea. Those who had done wickedness, all the human race who had turned to sin—the bodies of these floated like reeds.

"The ship was borne to the country of Nizir, and came to rest on the mountains of Nizir. On the seventh day afterward, I sent forth a dove, and it departed. And the dove flew away, and sought a place of rest; but it found none, and it returned. I let loose a raven. The raven flew forth, and it saw the bodies on the water, and it ate them; and it wandered a great way off, and it returned not. I let go the animals to the four winds; I poured out a libation; I built an altar on the summit of the mountain."

There can be no question of coincidence here. This account of the flood dates back only to about 700 B.C., but it is a copy of a Sumerian text that is perhaps 2000 years older—definitely far more ancient than the Bible of the Hebrews. The story of Noah as it appears in *Genesis* is almost certainly an adaptation of the old Sumerian myth.

It appears, too, that the flood itself was not simply a

legend. In 1929, the British archaeologist Leonard Woolley was excavating the Sumerian city of Ur, one of the oldest in all of Mesopotamia. In the depths of the ruin, at a level perhaps 6000 years old, Woolley came upon a thick layer of flood-deposited clay—*with signs of human settlement below it!* "No ordinary rising of the rivers would leave behind it anything approaching the bulk of this clay bank," Woolley wrote. "Eight feet of sediment imply a very great depth of water, and the flood which deposited it must have been of a magnitude unparallelled in local history."

So the city of Ur—and the whole lower valley of the Tigris and Euphrates, probably—was devastated by a terrible flood in the dim, time-misted past. To the inhabitants of the region, it must have seemed as though the whole world had been inundated. A myth grew, in the centuries that followed, of a vast deluge sent to punish the wicked, and of a virtuous man who escaped destruction and carried on the human race.

In one form, this myth found its way into the Bible that the priests of the Hebrews wrote, perhaps as early as 1300 B.C., thousands of years after the flood itself. In another form, the story was inscribed on clay tablets in the library of grim Sennacherib—and was found there, 2500 years later, by Austen Henry Layard and Hormuzd Rassam, to be translated twenty years later by George Smith!

Layard, in 1850, spent a few days examining his spectacular cache of tablets, and then floated down the river to Nimroud, where he confronted a modern deluge himself. The waters had spread over the plain, and part of the village of Nimroud, at the foot of the mound, had been destroyed. "The mud walls of my own house were falling in. The roof was supported by a few rude beams, and the

rooms with their furniture were deep in mud and silt. . . .
The center of the plain of Nimroud was now a large lake,
and the cultivated fields were overspread with slime."

Work was still proceeding calmly on the mound itself,
high above the flood waters. New trenches had been opened
along the brick platform that underlay all the Nimroud palaces, and a small temple had come to light, its main gate
flanked by two more of the giant winged lions, sixteen and
a half feet high and fifteen feet long. Within were an assortment of remarkable reliefs carved on limestone slabs,
and important inscriptions of the early Assyrian king Assurnasirpal. A second temple—and more winged lions—
were discovered a few days later.

Spring was ending, now. Well aware of the fury of a
Mesopotamian summer, Layard halted his Nimroud work,
and returned to Kouyunjik to begin his annual springtime
task of packing things up for shipment to England. His job
was complicated by the presence in Mosul of several English tourists, who had to be shown politely through Kouyunjik, at the expense of some days' work.

But as July came, and Mosul entered "the eye of the
summer," the tourists vanished from the scene. Layard's
own team began to suffer from the heat too. Cooper, the
sickly artist, was the first to succumb, and Layard sent him
off to a monastery in the hills to recuperate. Dr. Sandwith
found the climate too much for him, and headed for cooler
country shortly afterward. Layard and Hormuzd Rassam
struggled on alone to complete the packing operation.

Eventually they, too, came down with fever, but
"fortunately," Layard tells us, "our attacks did not coin-
cide." He and Rassam were sick on alternate days, it seems,
so there was always one of them up and about to supervise
the delicate packing job. By July 11, 1850, everything was

on its way down the river to Basra. Layard could be well satisfied with the results, as he brought to a close the first season of his second expedition. Not only had he found a wealth of new sculptured slabs and winged colossi, but he had made the pivotal discovery of Sennacherib's library. After the last raft had departed, Layard, feverish and half delirious, hurried out of Mosul for the cool comforts of the mountains of Kurdistan.

XV

LAYARD GOES TO BABYLON

When Layard returned to his excavations, at the summer's end, he found that his workmen had reopened the trenches at Kouyunjik and had ventured deep into the palace of Assurbanipal, near Sennacherib's. New sculptured slabs had been found, and Layard worked through the middle of October to pack them for shipment. It was a ticklish job, since Assurbanipal's palace had been put to the torch by its ancient invaders, and its walls had split into a thousand fragments in the heat. Layard painstakingly numbered each fragment so that they could be restored by the experts of the British Museum.

At length, nearly a hundred more cases of antiquities waited by the banks of the Tigris for shipment to Basra. Winter was drawing near, now, and Layard knew it would be a time of cold and rainy weather at Mosul. It was an ideal season for exploring the still untouched mounds of southern Mesopotamia, however. Layard decided to accompany his sculptures to Baghdad by raft, and then to examine Babylon and other lost cities of the south.

On October 18, he left Mosul, accompanied by Hormuzd Rassam and a picked party of trained Jebour workmen. After a two-day stop at Nimroud, the expedition continued southward, past Qalah Shergat toward Baghdad. For Layard, it meant reliving his raft trip with Mitford of ten years before—the wonder-filled journey down the river, marred at the very end when Layard slipped from the raft and took a dunking in the Tigris.

There were no such mishaps this time. Layard arrived —dry and well-groomed—at Baghdad on October 26, and was welcomed warmly by the British officials there. The ruins of Babylon were twenty-five miles away, at Hillah. But the Arabs around Baghdad were in revolt just then, and Layard was forced to delay his expedition to Hillah until December 5.

It would not have been like Layard to waste the month of involuntary delay. He dug into a few mounds not far from the gates of Baghdad, on the east bank of the Tigris, and found some crude statues of Ishtar, the Assyrian Venus, and one or two vases and rings. At length the rebellion was quelled, and Layard—down with a touch of fever once again—finally rode out to Hillah.

Layard had visited the site of Nebuchadnezzar's once-great city in 1840, but had had time only for a quick inspection. And, too, he was inexperienced in the ways of ruined cities then. Now, after five years of fruitful toil in Assyria, he hoped to add to his laurels by digging up Babylon.

There was no problem in finding the city. The site had never been lost—it had even retained the old name, as "Babel"—and it was plainly visible, an uninterrupted line of mounds running for nearly three miles through the desert. Fragments of pottery and colorful glazed bricks were strewn everywhere over the surface of the mounds.

Layard remained in Hillah for two weeks, supervising the excavations. He was badly troubled by malarial attacks, and the uneasy truce between the desert Arabs and the Baghdad authorities added to the uncertainties of the situation. Layard made his first excavation in the biggest mound, the one that still bore the name of Babel. Claudius Rich had noticed a subterranean passage, about thirteen feet square, leading into the mound, and Layard soon redis-covered it. In the forty years since Rich's visit, the entrance to the passage had become clogged with earth and had to be cleared.

Layard entered. Within was a coffin containing a well-preserved skeleton, and some square stones inscribed with the cuneiform-written name and titles of Nebuchadnezzar, King of Babylon. The coffin, though, seemed fairly recent, dating from a time well after the fall of Babylon.

Other trenches elsewhere in the mound produced little of real interest—some arrowheads, a few glass bottles, some attractive pottery, and a soapstone jug. All these things, though, appeared to date from the time of the Greek oc-cupation of Babylon, and even later, perhaps as late as A.D. 600. Of actual Babylonian relics, nothing but bricks stamped with Nebuchadnezzar's name emerged. The work-men unearthed what Layard called "a confused heap of ruin and standing masonry." And, he noted, "The enormous accumulation of loose rubbish above them, not a hard, compact mass, as at Nineveh, but continually crumbling and falling in, exposed the men to a risk scarcely warranted by the results of their labors."

Layard's Babylon excavations were unsuccessful. His own verdict was, "I much doubt whether even more ex-tensive excavations would lead to any important discov-eries."

The reason for this disappointment, he knew, lay in the difference between Assyrian and Babylonian geography. To the north, the builders of the Assyrian palaces had had access to quarries of limestone. But Babylon had risen in an alluvial plain—that is, on land deposited by rivers in recent times. There was no building stone available nearby, only rich, thick clay.

And so Babylon was built of brick, not stone. For special buildings, kiln-baked bricks of great durability were used, but the average Babylonian construction was done with bricks made simply of mud that had dried in the sun. With the passage of centuries, these bricks crumbled and decomposed, and it became almost impossible to tell where debris left off and building walls began.

This explains why Layard failed at Babylon. His vigorous, impatient nature balked at the task of patiently picking through mounds of mud. Nor did he have the experience necessary to identify Babylonian buildings. He saw the job of excavating Babylon as a thankless one. And he remarked to another archaeologist, Fresnel, "There will be nothing to be hoped for from the site of Babylon except with a parliamentary vote of £25,000, and if ever this sum should be voted, I would solicit the favor of not being charged with its application."

Almost fifty years would pass before anyone could accept the challenge of Babylon. In 1899, a German team under Dr. Robert Koldewey began work on the site, using precision techniques of excavation that would have astonished Layard. Methodically they peeled the debris from Nebuchadnezzar's city the way one would skin an onion. Working with tweezers and camel's-hair brush as much as with picks and spades, the German team labored until 1917. Koldewey's work at Babylon is one of the glories of archaeology. Before he was through, he had revealed not only the palace of Nebuchadnezzar but the Tower of Babel itself, the Hanging Gardens that were one of the wonders of the ancient world, and the Sacred Way of Babylon, perhaps the grandest street ever built.

After his disappointment at Babylon, Layard headed

onward to examine the mounds further to the south. He was now entering, though he could not have known it, the oldest settled part of Mesopotamia. Here, south of Babylon, the Sumerian cities had risen, four thousand years before Christ: Ur and Nippur, Uruk and Lagash and Eridu.

On January 15, 1851, Layard and his party left Hillah. It was a bright, intensely cold day, with a biting north wind sweeping across the plain. Hormuzd Rassam, fever-stricken, remained behind in Baghdad.

Layard headed due east at first, toward the center of the Mesopotamian desert. "The long belt of feathery palms bordering the Euphrates for many and many a mile," he writes, "and broken here and there by a dome or a minaret, became gradually less distinct, until it was but a faint black line edging the horizon. About six miles from Hillah we found ourselves amidst moving sand-hills, extending far and wide on all sides. They were just high enough to shut out the view of the surrounding country. The fine sand shifts with every breeze, and the wrinkled heaps are like the rippled surface of a lake."

Layard's first objective was the huge mound of Niffar, about fifty miles below Hillah on the edge of a great swamp. After visiting with the Arabs who lived in the marsh on floating huts, Layard attacked the mound itself.

The mound fell into four distinct sections, each separated from the others by deep ravines. At the northeast corner was a high cone that held the remains of a tower of sun-dried bricks, stamped with cuneiform characters. Layard put workmen to digging there, and at the other three segments of the mound.

The first discoveries were human burials of comparatively recent date. Then came vases and jars of earthenware, some glazed and others plain, and broken bowls. On the second day, the workmen found fragments of highly glazed blue pottery, and then, two days later, a coffin of the same material. Within was a human body, which—a familiar refrain—"crumbled to dust almost as soon as exposed to the air."

Dozens of these pottery coffins came to light, until Layard had found more than a hundred. They were so fragile he could not remove any of them, and he had the same problem with the bodies they contained. "Sometimes, as the lid was carefully removed, I could almost distinguish the body, wrapped in its grave clothes, and still lying in its narrow resting-place. But no sooner did the outer air reach the empty crust of humanity than it fell away into dust, leaving only the skull and great bones of the arms and legs to show what these now empty cases had once contained."

Continued digging produced nothing but coffins, so that Layard began to think the entire mound was one vast cemetery. Despite the fragility of the coffins and their contents, Layard thought that they dated from the early centuries of the Christian era. The ancient city of the mound was somewhere beneath, but he could not reach it. Perhaps it was not there at all. Discouraged, Layard wrote, "With the exception of a few massive foundations, and the bricks bearing a cuneiform superscription, I much doubt whether anything found at Niffar was of the true Babylonian period." And he added pessimistically, "On the whole, I am much inclined to question whether extensive excavations carried on at Niffar would produce any very important or interesting results."

After Niffar, Layard's next stop was intended to be the mound of Warka, which we know today is the site of the

Sumerian city of Uruk. Another British traveler, W. K. Loftus, had excavated at Warka for three weeks in 1850, and had found inscribed clay tablets, glazed pottery, tombs of a late period, and other minor oddments. Layard hoped to continue Loftus' work. Unhappily, the Arab tribe of Montefik, which occupied the region around Warka, was in a state of civil war, defying all outside authority as brother massacred brother. So violent was the scene that Layard was unable to follow through on his projected trip to Warka. Had he gone, though, the results would probably have been much the same as at Babylon and Niffar.

He went back and camped at Niffar for a while, but, he writes, "The dampness of the soil upon which my tent was pitched, and the unwholesome air of the surrounding marshes, brought on a severe attack of pleurisy and fever. I was soon unable to move from my bed, and was reduced at length to a state of extreme weakness."

It occurred to him, though, to treat himself with a liniment usually reserved for horses. "Notwithstanding the severity of the remedy it gave me immediate relief." On January 28, Hormuzd Rassam joined him at Niffar, and Layard decided to return with him to Baghdad for medical care.

A cold, dismal rainfall commenced and would not end for four days. Water rose from the marsh and leaked into their tents. Word came that the Arabs around Baghdad were again rebelling, and Layard saw that if he did not return at once, he might be cut off by hostile tribesmen.

On February 2, though still weak with fever, he broke camp and headed for Baghdad. The following day, a large body of horsemen appeared in the distance, just as Layard and his party had reached the ruin called Zibbliyah. Ascending the mound, Layard and his companions prepared to defend themselves. The horsemen, however, passed on in another direction, and there was no attack. As one might expect, Layard took advantage of the stop to make a quick inspection of Zibbliyah, sick as he was, before continuing!

Layard rode onward, fourteen hours a day. His workmen, not having horses, followed along on foot, and he waited in a small village the next day for them to catch up with him. They arrived finally, bedraggled and almost naked, for on their way they had ventured into the tents of some Arabs in search of water, and had been robbed of their scanty possessions.

Though he had hardly strength enough to mount his horse, Layard forced himself onward, and shortly neared Baghdad. He rode into town with Rassam at his side, and tells us, in a phrase characteristic of his whole career, "I had but just strength left me to reach the gates of Baghdad. Once in the city, under the friendly care of Dr. Hyslop, I soon recovered my health, and was ready to start on fresh adventures."

XVI

FAREWELL TO MESOPOTAMIA

After recovering at Baghdad, Layard set out at once for his headquarters in Mosul. An Arab tribe, the Shammar, had started to move northward toward their summer pasture, and he arranged to travel under their protection through the desert and along the western bank of the Tigris to Mosul.

In return for the favor of escorting him, Sahiman, the Arab chieftain, asked Layard to obtain permission from the Pasha of Baghdad for the Shammar to drive their camels and flocks through the suburbs of Baghdad, instead of taking a longer and more difficult route through the marshes. The Pasha agreed to this, and gave Layard a guarantee that the Arabs would be allowed to enter the city unmolested.

No sooner did they enter the gates, though, than they were fallen upon by the city's troops. The Arabs fled, abandoning nearly eight hundred camels.

Layard was furious at the treacherous act. "The Turkish authorities declared that it was an accident beyond their control, and at length adopted means to recover the stolen camels. It was, however, with some difficulty that I was able to find Sahiman, and then to induce him to return to Baghdad."

Not until February 27 were the camels recovered and the Arabs ready to depart. The journey took some days, but was without major incident. Layard stopped off to visit the mound of Qalah Shergat once again as he traveled northward. Under Rassam's direction, workmen were again excavating there, but little had been found except fragments of a winged limestone bull, part of a statue in black stone, and pieces of a large inscribed copper slab. Perhaps spoiled by his easy successes at Nimroud and Kouyunjik, Layard decided, "I am inclined to doubt whether an edifice containing any number of sculptures or inscriptions ever existed on that platform." Once again, it remained for later and better trained archaeologists to prove him wrong.

That night, Layard and his Arab escorts camped in the jungle north of the ruins. They were visited by fifteen men of the Albou Mohammed tribe of Arabs, who admitted with wonderful sincerity that they were thieves out on a raiding party. Layard writes, "As the tribe does not bear a very good character for honesty, and as it might have struck our guests that they had no need of going further to fulfill the object of their journey, we violated the duties of hospitality, and put some of them in irons for the night, as a guarantee for the good conduct of the rest."

Soon after, Layard was back at Kouyunjik. He found an artist named Bell waiting for him there. Bell had been sent out from England to replace Cooper, whose health had given way entirely and who had been forced to return to England the previous summer.

Layard promptly put the new man to work sketching the latest discoveries at Kouyunjik. But Bell's career in archaeology was short and tragic. A few months later, at the nearby site of Bavian where Sennacherib had left an important rock inscription, Bell decided to cool off with a dip in the Gomel River. More experienced hands warned him about the treacherous currents, but Bell was confident of his abilities as a swimmer. He entered the river and was promptly swept away, and Layard had to write to the British Museum for a third artist. He got one, too, a young man named Hodder who turned out to be incompetent.

During Layard's absence in the south, work had continued at Kouyunjik, and more and yet more chambers of Sennacherib's palace had been uncovered. The mound seemed to contain endless treasure. Nearing the end of his work at Kouyunjik, Layard summed up his activities as follows:

"In this magnificent edifice [the palace of Sennacherib] I had opened no less than seventy-one halls, chambers, and passages, whose walls, almost without an exception, had been panelled with slabs of sculptured alabaster recording the wars, the triumphs, and the great deeds of the Assyrian king. By a rough calculation, about 9880 feet, or nearly two miles, of bas-reliefs, with twenty-seven portals formed by colossal winged bulls and lion-sphinxes, were uncovered in that part alone of the building explored during my researches. The greatest length of the excavations was about 720 feet, the greatest breadth about 600 feet. The pavement of the chambers was from 20 to 35 feet below the surface of the mound."

All during his years at Mosul, Layard had been contemplating hopefully the sacred mound of Nebbi Yunus. Because it was supposed to be the site of the tomb of the prophet Jonah, a superstition which Layard regarded as "a mere fable," it had been impossible for him to attack the mound with pick and spade.

A bit of cleverness allowed Layard to make at least a superficial examination of Nebbi Yunus. What happened was that a villager who lived atop the mound decided to make *serdaubs*, or underground summer apartments, for himself. He let it be known that he needed workmen to do the digging beneath the foundations of his house.

Layard sent his foreman, Toma Shishman, to see the man. "Let us dig your *serdaubs* for you," Toma Shishman told him. "It will cost you nothing—but you must give us any relics and sculptures we uncover."

It was thus agreed, and Layard's workmen crossed the river and began to dig. Excavation for relics on Nebbi Yunus was considered sacrilege, but building *serdaubs* was perfectly all right, and who would notice if the workmen accidentally dug a trifle too far?

After a few days of digging, Layard's men came to the walls of a chamber, paneled with inscribed but unsculptured alabaster slabs. Studying the inscription, Layard was able to read the name of Esarhaddon, Sennacherib's son. But he could not dare go further without risking the wrath of the villagers.

Layard's guess that Nebbi Yunus contained a palace of Esarhaddon was confirmed some time later, when another villager of the mound, digging the foundations of his house, came upon a pair of colossal human-headed winged bulls, and two figures of the Mesopotamian hero Gilgamesh slaying lions. Layard was not in Mosul at the time, and the Turkish authorities moved in and seized the sculptures. They were sent off to Constantinople to form the nucleus of a Turkish collection of Assyrian antiquities, and later proved to be of the time of Esarhaddon.

Layard was nearing the end of this second season of work. Little remained for him to do. He visited a mound called Shereef-Khan, three miles to the north of Kouyunjik, and discovered Assyrian ruins there, but did not excavate extensively. At Nimroud, a few Arabs were still at work, but the most recent finds had not been of very great interest. Kouyunjik was still obviously full of treasures, but as the warm weather approached it became inadvisable to continue.

Late in April, 1851, Layard began to prepare for his return to England. "Once more," he writes, "I was about to leave the ruins amidst which I had spent so many happy hours, and to which I was bound by so many pleasant and solemn ties."

Since he was taking with him a valuable collection of bronzes and other small objects found in the ruins, Layard decided it was best to travel under the protection of some important figure. It happened that Abde Pasha, who had been governor of Baghdad, was being transferred by the Sultan to the governorship of Diarbekir, a city to the north-west in Kurdistan. Layard made arrangements to travel from Mosul to Diarbekir as a member of Abde Pasha's party.

"At length, after the usual Eastern delays," Layard tells us, "the Pasha arrived at Mosul. He remained en-camped outside the town for two or three days, and during that time visited the excavations, his curiosity having been excited by the description he had received of the wondrous idols dug out of the ruins. He marvelled at what he saw, as a Turk marvels at strange things which he can neither understand nor explain. It would be in vain to speak to him of the true objects of such researches, the knowledge they impart, the lessons they teach, or the thoughts they beget."

Layard had long since abandoned any attempt to explain the motives behind his excavations. The Turks and Arabs never really grasped the value of expending so much time, energy and money on a quest for things of the dead past.

For twelve years, he had risked life and limb to seek that which he required not. He had roved the mountains of Persia and the blazing deserts of Mesopotamia. He had suffered cold and heat, rain and wind and the fury of the sun. He had been robbed and cheated, and many times threatened with violent death. He had toiled long hours to strip the covering from the shattered palaces of the fallen mighty.

Why?

We know why, you and I. But Layard could never have explained to the Turks of Mosul that a hunger for knowledge drove him ever onward. He simply smiled, and left them to draw their own conclusions, and if they thought he was a madman, so it would be.

His time in Assyria was at an end. On April 28, 1851, Layard "bid a last farewell to my faithful Arab friends, and with a heavy heart turned from the ruins of ancient Nineveh."

XVII

Ey the summer of 1851, Layard was back in England. He knew that there was plenty still to do in the mounds of Assyria, and so we would guess that he would have done as he did four years before on returning—request funds to allow him to undertake a third expedition.

Strangely, he did not. It is one of the mysteries of Layard's career that he retired from archaeology at this point. He was 34 years old, had spent a dozen years abroad and six of them in brilliant excavations in the mounds of Assyria. Now, with such abrupt suddenness that it startles us, Layard rang down the curtain on his career in archaeology.

We do not know why. Although he left us documentation on almost every stage of his life, he is vague about his change of heart. Certainly his second expedition had been every bit as successful as the first, even more so, and his fame as an archaeologist was great. His autobiography mentions "private troubles and anxieties, combined with frequent attacks of fever," that served to convince him he should not return to Mosul.

And so, in November 1851, we find him writing to his friend Ross, who still remained at Mosul:

"My plans are still so uncertain that I cannot give you the slightest idea of them. I shall certainly not leave England again if I can help it, but I may be forced to do so, as, at present at any rate, I have no means of making ends meet without some employment. I shall make a desperate effort not to return to the East, not even to Stamboul [Constantinople], which does not agree with me in any way—the climate always disagrees with me, and I can find neither books nor society. I should like to get into Parliament in England, and think that, if once there, I could push my way."

In this letter we can see the beginning of Layard's transformation from the bold, endlessly dashing young man of Nineveh to the white-bearded patriarch that his later portraits show him to have become. His career of adventure was over, after a dozen magnificent years, and now he turned to public life, to politics and diplomacy.

First there was a book to write, though. Through most of 1851 and early 1852, Layard was busy with literary endeavors. He produced a two-volume sequel to *Nineveh and Its Remains*, called *Discoveries in the Ruins of Nineveh and Babylon: With Travels in Armenia, Kurdistan and the Desert: Being the Result of a Second Expedition Undertaken for the Trustees of the British Museum.* John Murray published it in 1853.

Although most sequels notoriously do not have the impact of the original book, *Nineveh and Babylon* was eagerly devoured by the British reading public. It lacked some of the vigor and gusto of the earlier book, since Layard on his second expedition had been mature and publicly sponsored, where he had been working in the dark on the earlier trip. Uncertainty had given way to confident assurance, and the result was a less exciting, though better-informed, book. In a letter to Ross in July 1853, only a few months after publication, Layard wrote, "You will, I am sure, be glad to hear that my last work has had a great success. Nearly twelve thousand copies have already been sold, and three thousand more will be shortly printed."

There were other books to prepare, too. 1851 saw the publication of Layard's copies of cuneiform inscriptions, and the abridged edition of *Nineveh and Its Remains*. Then came a second ten-guinea folio of plates, in 1853, called *The Palace of Sennacherib: Monuments of Nineveh, Second Series*.

Layard was also casting about for ways to begin his political career. Under the British Parliamentary system, it was and still is not necessary for a candidate to Parliament to reside in the district he hopes to represent. It is possible to run as a candidate from any part of England, and, if defeated, to run immediately in another district.

British Parliamentary elections are held whenever the Prime Minister, who is the head of the party in power, feels that he no longer commands the support of a majority in Parliament. No Parliament can remain in office more than five years under any circumstances; an election must be called at the end of that period if there has been none, regardless of the strength of the majority power.

England was then in a time of political confusion. For a century and a half, two great political parties, the Whigs and the Tories (or Conservatives) had alternated in governing the country. But in the general political ferment of the middle years of the nineteenth century, both parties were badly split. Within a few years the Whigs, who had been the more liberal-minded of the two parties, would disappear entirely. In their place would arise the Liberal Party, made up of the remnants of the Whigs in coalition with some of the more liberal Tories. The Tories would survive as a party, but for many years they would not have enough strength to take national power.

Layard's own political sympathies were strongly liberal. He had seen enough injustice and corruption in his years abroad to teach him the importance of honest government on behalf of all the citizens, not merely the richest ones. He was in favor of sweeping political reforms in England that would take some of the power away from the upper classes and allow workingmen a greater voice in their government.

When Layard returned from the Orient, the new Liberal Party was in office, after a disastrous split in the then-ruling Tories in 1846. The Prime Minister was Lord John Russell. Early in 1852, a vacancy developed in the post of Under-Secretary of State for Foreign Affairs. Normally, this office would have gone to some member of Parliament.

But Layard was riding the crest of his Nineveh fame, and Lord Granville, the Foreign Secretary, chose him for the job. The departure from custom caused some eyebrow-lifting, but Layard was so popular that no one seriously objected to the appointment.

Almost immediately after Layard took office, Lord John Russell's government ran into Parliamentary difficulties and had to resign. The Tories came briefly into power, with Lord Derby as Prime Minister. However, Lord Malmesbury, the new Foreign Secretary, asked Layard to stay in office for a while.

The Tories did not have sufficient strength in Parliament to remain in control. In July 1852, Parliament was dissolved and a General Election called. Layard thus got his first chance to run for office.

He was given the nomination as Liberal candidate for the town of Aylesbury. Aylesbury had long been represented by Tories, but Layard's father had lived there for a while, giving Layard a family connection with the place, and, besides, the discoverer of Nineveh was one of England's most widely known figures at the time. Layard's backer, in his nominating speech, recommended him as a man "who had brought to light with extraordinary spirit Ancient History, and that which was interesting to religious-minded men—a man of powerful mind, of indomitable courage, and lofty principles."

Layard won easily. On July 9, 1852, he described the victory celebration in a letter:

"I never saw such a scene of triumph as our . . . procession. Every window full of well-dressed ladies, showering down bouquets of flowers, sending cakes and wine, waving flags, etc. etc. The procession must have extended half a mile. Women brought their babies, and carried them before us. It was a complete triumph and most gratifying."

The man who had once entered Baghdad barefoot and another time soaking wet now took his seat in the House of Commons, in November 1852. The Tories under Lord Derby were once again in power, but only for a month. In December, Lord Derby and the Tories had to resign after a bitter financial debate, and the Whig-Liberal coalition took over. The new Prime Minister was Lord Aberdeen.

This was the same Lord Aberdeen who had been Foreign Minister a decade before, when Layard had been working for Sir Stratford Canning in Constantinople. As one of the young, vigorous new Liberals, Layard had reason to hope that Lord Aberdeen would name him to some important position in the new government. Trouble was stirring in the Near East, and it would have been logical to give a man with Layard's particular experience a policy-making post in the Foreign Office.

Lord Aberdeen, though, had been the man who blocked

Layard's hopes of becoming a member of the staff of the British Embassy in Constantinople in the early 1840's, and perhaps he remembered his old prejudice against Layard. Whatever the reason, Layard was given no job. He wrote in discouragement to a relative, "After keeping me in suspense all this while, they have decided, I understand, that I am to have nothing. I have not received one word, however, from any of the great people on the subject, either by way of explanation or otherwise."

It seemed to Layard that there was no future for him in Parliament so long as Lord Aberdeen was in charge of things. At that time, members of Parliament received no salary, and he could not afford to remain in office without hope of receiving a government post.

At this depressing point, an old friend came to Layard's rescue—Sir Stratford Canning, now bearing the title of Lord Stratford de Redcliffe. Lord Stratford invited Layard to take employment with him once again at Constantinople.

So—somewhat to his own surprise—Layard found himself leaving Parliament and turning eastward once again. By April 1853, he was in Constantinople, holding no official appointment but serving in Lord Stratford's pay.

It was a turbulent time in the East. Russia and Turkey were snarling at one another, and the tensions were mounting that soon would explode into the bloody fury of the Crimean War. Lord Stratford hoped to avoid the outbreak of war. He dreamed of a day when corrupt, decaying Turkey would be broken into a number of independent states, as finally happened after World War I, but he did not want Turkey's reform to come about as the after-effect of a war with Russia.

The friction between the two powers grew more heated, and Russia became more menacing. Despite Lord Stratford's efforts, war soon became inevitable. Layard was on hand to watch the developing situation. But he was frustrated because Lord Stratford did not give him more responsibility. Writing sadly home that he had nothing to do and might just as well be in Tasmania, Layard reluctantly left Constantinople after a month and returned to England.

Lord Aberdeen, who for years had been supporting Russia in her quarrels with Turkey, failed to see the danger of war in the East now. Layard resumed his seat in Parliament and tried desperately to awaken the government to the critical nature of the situation. Russia's actions were becoming increasingly objectionable. In July, Layard declared, "I will venture to state that, in the whole history of the intercourse of nations, acts so unjustifiable, so outrageous, so dangerous as those which have been committed within the last three months have never previously been committed in Europe."

Layard was a voice crying in the wilderness. He begged Parliament to devote some time to a discussion of the Turkish situation, but more than a month went by before the matter came under attention.

Some members of Parliament accused Layard of being bloodthirsty, hot-headed, eager for war. He replied that he simply believed Russia should be stopped from gobbling up Turkey piecemeal, and that Britain was the only power strong enough to restore the eastern situation to a state of calmness. "As a result of our inaction," Layard declared, "Turkey has received a fatal blow. The Russian occupation of the Principalities is accepted, and Great Britain is regarded by the weaker states who look to her support as

181

helpless against Russian encroachments." And he concluded his speech, "I have witnessed all these circumstances with extreme pain and regret. The day will come when we shall see the fatal error we have committed, and repent a policy against which, as a humble member of this House, I can only record my solemn protest."

Layard was cheered by many members of Parliament, but there was no budging Lord Aberdeen. As late as February 1854—a month before the war broke out—Aberdeen could manage to write, "I still say that war is not inevitable, unless, indeed, we are determined to have it; which, for all I know, may be the case."

The Crimean War began in March, with France and Great Britain allied with Turkey against the Russians. It was a mismanaged, horridly botched, and costly little war, whose best-remembered episode is the suicidal Charge of the Light Brigade. Perhaps, if Layard had been listened to, some of the casualties of that war might have been avoided.

But Layard had not been able to get his point home in time. All he succeeded in doing was widening the breach between himself and Lord Aberdeen. He was in the awkward position of having criticized the head of his own party. So long as Lord Aberdeen was Prime Minister, Layard knew there was not the faintest chance of his own political advancement.

Since there was nothing he could accomplish in England, Layard decided to observe the progress of the war. He therefore made yet another trip East, and spent some months watching the incredible bungling and confusion that both sides were displaying. The short journal he kept of his observations in the Crimea vividly shows the ill-coordinated manner in which the war was conducted.

So outrageous was the way the war was fought that

the English suffered staggeringly heavy losses, and there was great public outcry against the government of Lord Aberdeen. In January 1855, Aberdeen's generals and admirals had made him look so foolish that the Prime Minister had to resign.

The new Prime Minister was Lord Palmerston, who was friendly toward Layard. Under Palmerston, the war was brought to a fairly rapid conclusion, and by February 1856, peace was being negotiated.

Layard, back in England, had a new political target. He became a leading advocate of governmental reform. The Crimean War, he argued, had graphically demonstrated the incompetence of the old system, where high posts were awarded on the basis of noble birth, political influence or wealth, rather than on merit. He called for a complete overhaul of the government system, and did not hesitate even to attack the new Prime Minister, Lord Palmerston.

Layard had now completed the process of cutting himself off from his own party. He was too liberal, too outspoken even for the Liberals. Disraeli, who had had such an influence on the teen-aged Layard years ago, was now an influential member of the Tories, and tried to tempt Layard to cross party lines and become a Conservative. But if there was no room for him among the Liberals, there was certainly none with the Tories, and Layard declined the invitation.

It was now 1857. Five years had gone by since the last election, and Parliament was dissolved. Layard decided not to run again. The House of Commons was not a comfortable place for him. Besides, the old itch to travel was upon him.

In 1851 he had written, "I shall certainly not leave

England again if I can help it." But Layard had not been born a stay-at-home. In 1853 he had gone to Constantinople, in 1854 to the Crimea, and now, in 1857, he departed for another land of his childhood dreams—India.

India was a British possession, and was then being racked by a terrible uprising known as the Sepoy Mutiny. Ever alert for a dangerous situation, Layard entered India while the revolt was still going on. As an exponent of governmental reform, he was interested in seeing whether the mutiny had been the result of misgovernment by the British.

This was, he found, the case. In a letter home dated January 13, 1858, after the suppression of the revolt, he wrote, "We have had a narrow escape in this part of India. Indeed, the sympathy of the populations appears to have been with the rebels in all parts of the Peninsula. The sooner people in England open their eyes to the truth . . . the better." And he observed, "We have done nothing to form a bond of sympathy between the conquered people and their rulers, or to create mutual interests. The people we govern are treated like a distinct race, inferior to us—more, indeed, as if they were of a lower order of creatures; not always actually unkindly, but with that sort of kindness which would be shown to a pet animal."

Naturally, Layard took the opportunity to visit the monuments of ancient India as well as to observe the current state of the country. He toured ruins and temples, and was struck by their "imposing and religious effect"—though he could not resist remarking that "as art, these works rank low, and are inferior to all prior and contemporary works of Italy, or of Greece, or even of Egypt and Assyria."

Layard returned to England by way of Italy, where he

devoted some months to the study of Italian paintings of the Middle Ages. He was developing a new fascination for this period of art (or, rather, reviving an old one, for his father had taken him to the museums of Florence many years before) which was gradually ousting his interest in Assyria.

Back home, in 1859, Layard tried to return to Parliament. He was defeated by twenty votes as a candidate from York, but in December 1860 he ran again, this time from the Southwark district of London, and defeated his Conservative opponent by 1195 votes.

There had been several changes of government since Layard's departure from Parliament in 1857. Lord Palmerston's Liberal government had given way, in 1858, to the Tories under Lord Derby. In 1859, Palmerston returned as Prime Minister and held that post until 1865.

Layard had had his differences with Palmerston over the question of reform, but these were patched over. Lord John Russell, who had been Prime Minister from 1846 to 1852, was now Foreign Minister, and he offered Layard, in June 1861, the post of Under-Secretary for Foreign Affairs. This was the job Layard had held for a few months in 1852, before the beginning of his career in Parliament.

Layard was a valuable member of the new government, and was in the thick of many important political debates. When a General Election was called in July 1865, Layard was re-elected to Parliament without opposition. Soon after, Lord Palmerston died at 81, and Lord John Russell returned as Prime Minister.

A year later, the Russell government was defeated while trying to pass a reform measure, and Layard had to resign along with the other Liberals. The Tories under Lord Derby seesawed back into control of the government, and when Derby retired in 1868 Benjamin Disraeli at last achieved the ambition he had boasted of more than thirty years before, and became Prime Minister.

In November of that year, the Conservative government fell. A new election was called, and the Liberals were swept back into power. Layard was elected once again. The new Prime Minister was the great Liberal leader, William Gladstone, who gave Layard a job, not in the Foreign Office this time, but as Chief Commissioner of Works.

It was a strange assignment for the discoverer of Nineveh. Layard was responsible for the maintenance and construction of public buildings. As a man with some taste in art, Layard tried to introduce Italian ideas of beauty and nobility into English public works. But this was the heyday of Victorian architecture, and Layard was unable to put his viewpoints into operation. After quarreling bitterly with a Treasury official over the expense of redecorating the Parliament buildings, Layard was glad to be given a new assignment, and in 1869 he was named by Prime Minister Gladstone as British Ambassador to Spain.

And so Layard's stormy, controversial career in Parliament came to an end and he took up the rank of an ambassador. The British comic weekly, *Punch*, ran an amusing poem called "Don Layardos in Madrid," accompanied by a cartoon showing a thick-bearded, solemn Layard riding into the Spanish capital on the back of a smirking Assyrian winged bull, whose features were suspiciously similar to those of Queen Victoria.

Layard had now become a married man. Through most of his life he had been so busy roaming the wild places of the world, digging up ancient cities, and furthering his political career, that so conventional a subject as marriage never seemed to cross his mind. In middle age, though, he began to regret what he called "a sad solitary life," and when he was fifty-two he astonished his friends by taking a wife.

She was twenty-five-year-old Enid Guest, one of the eight children of Layard's cousin, Lady Charlotte Schreiber. For many years, Layard had been fond of Enid's younger and prettier sister, Blanche, and it appears to have come as something of a surprise to everyone when, in January 1869, he asked Enid to be his wife. She was a tall, stately woman—taller than the stocky Layard—who had been brought up in a primly correct way. Layard had one of London's finest jewelers make a bracelet for his bride out of Esarhaddon's signet ring. He also presented Enid with an elaborate necklace made out of cuneiform cylinders—a novel but perhaps not very elegant ornament! Though she was half his age, and genteel and refined where he was impulsive and high-spirited, Enid was a contented wife who remained devoted to Layard through the quarter century of their marriage.

Layard served in Spain for several years. In 1874, the Liberals lost power once again, and Disraeli's Conservatives regained the government. Although Layard was a member of the opposition party, Disraeli found a singularly appropriate job for him. Layard was named, in 1877, to be Her Majesty's Ambassador to Turkey. At the same time he was knighted as Sir Henry Layard.

It was a marvelous idea. Layard returned in triumph to the Near East, and took up residence in the Embassy at Constantinople—the selfsame Embassy where he had been so coolly and rudely received thirty-five years before, when, ragged and tanned, he had arrived with messages for Sir Stratford Canning. Layard was now sixty years old, distinguished and respectable, with an enormous white beard. His experiences in the Orient stood him in good stead during his four years in Constantinople, and he plunged with all his old fervor into the intrigues and tangled politics of the decaying Turkish Empire. But he did not show any revival of his interest in archaeology. It does not seem that he even visited the scenes of his old glories, the mounds of Assyria.

But he did revisit Damascus, where thirty-eight years before he had come sneaking into the city like a fugitive. Now he came as Queen Victoria's Ambassador to Turkey, and the city's governor and all his retinue marched several miles out of Damascus to greet the advancing Layard. Then, as the Ambassador continued toward the city, thousands of cheering men and women assembled to hail him. It was quite a contrast to his first arrival in Damascus in 1840!

In 1880, Layard retired from public life. He settled in Venice, and took up the study and collecting of Venetian painting. He wrote a number of magazine articles on historical and artistic subjects, and occupied himself with a revision and expansion of a standard textbook, Kugler's *Handbook of Painting: The Italian Schools.*

Layard also gave some thought to completing the record of his own life. First he dug out the notes of his travels from 1839 to 1845, and wrote a two-volume work, *Early Adventures,* which was published with great success in 1887. Although more than forty years had gone by, Layard was still able to write of those hair-raising escapades with his youthful dash and charm, and the book was a best-seller.

Next, Layard set down an autobiographical account of his life from childhood through the discovery of Nineveh, and set it aside to be published after his death. It finally appeared in 1903. He also wrote a further autobiography, taking his life from 1851 to his retirement, but this was such a revealing political document, with its inside view of the great Parliamentary figures of the time, that Layard decided it could not be published until all the individuals involved were dead. It never saw print.

In old age Layard, like many men, turned a trifle crusty and conservative. He thought the world was "tending to the ridiculous." It was not enough for young gentlemen to imitate Layard by going off on daring journeys to unknown places; young women were doing it too, and old Sir Henry found that shocking and bewildering. The wild modern idea that women should be allowed to vote and hold public office also struck him as incredible and absurd. Toward the end of his life, he quietly hoped that he might be given some high title—"Baron Layard of Nineveh," a friend suggested—but he had made too many political enemies in his stormy youth, and a peerage was not forthcoming.

In Venice, Layard and Enid celebrated their silver wedding anniversary in March 1894. "When I married," he wrote, "I could not have believed that I should reach my silver wedding. Well, I have been very fortunate, and I can say, what few married men can say, that my wife and I have never been separated for one single day and that we have never had a quarrel." Layard was in good health for a man of his age, but early in April he fell ill, and his doctor diagnosed the trouble as a malignant tumor. He returned to London for treatment, but little could be done. He died there on July 5, 1894, in his seventy-eighth year, having won everlasting fame as the discoverer of lost Nineveh.

XVIII

ASSYRIA AFTER LAYARD

Layard's spectacular success in Assyria set in motion an archaeological whirligig that is still going on in our own day. He had only scratched the surface, as he well knew, and after his abrupt retirement from the scene in 1851 there were many who were willing to carry on the work.

At Nimroud, Kouyunjik and Qalah Shergat, Hormuzd Rassam continued Layard's excavations from 1852 to 1854. Henry Rawlinson, who had returned to the Near East after publication of his famous book on Assyrian and Babylonian cuneiform, served as a kind of general coordinator for the various English excavations around Mosul.

The French, who had been inactive since Botta's departure, now returned to the field. An architect named Victor Place was named to re-open the French excavations at Khorsabad. The French government also provided Place with funds for what was vaguely termed, "A scientific and artistic expedition to Mesopotamia and Media."

Place interpreted this to mean that he had license to cut in on the English work at Nimroud and Kouyunjik. Paying a call on Rawlinson, Place asked to be allowed to dig at Kouyunjik, and Rawlinson generously marked out a portion of the mound where the French could work.

It was a noble gesture, but it was doomed to failure. Place and Rassam could not get along with one another at all. Working side by side at Kouyunjik, they quarreled fiercely, and Rassam refused to recognize Rawlinson's agreement with the Frenchman.

One of the things that troubled Rassam was that Place's workmen were approaching what Rassam suspected was the most promising part of the whole mound. This was the Palace of Assurbanipal, which Layard had just barely touched. Rassam, though an energetic and capable excavator, had a wide streak of vanity in his makeup, and it seemed unbearable to him that Rawlinson should have handed such a prize to his rival.

So one night late in 1853, while Place was off at Khorsabad, Rassam and his workmen quietly entered the French section of Kouyunjik and began to dig, "at the risk," Rassam writes, "of getting into hot water with Mr. Place."

That night Rassam came across a few sculptured slabs. Returning secretly the next night, he continued to dig, and after three or four hours' hard labor was "rewarded by the first grand discovery of a beautiful bas-relief in a perfect state of preservation, representing the king, who was afterward identified as Assurbanipal, standing in a chariot, about to start on a hunting expedition, and his attendants handing him the necessary weapons for the chase."

Rassam had found one of the masterpieces of Assyrian art—and further digging revealed something even more remarkable, a library of clay tablets that rivaled Sennacherib's library, which Layard had found.

Place hurried back from Khorsabad when he learned that the "gentleman's agreement" had been broken. Rassam stubbornly maintained that he had never agreed to Rawlinson's decision, and that he had priority in the mound by virtue of having been Layard's assistant. To Place's credit, he swallowed his chagrin, congratulated Rassam on his good fortune, and made no further claim to the mound. The library and sculptures of Assurbanipal are among the British Museum's proudest possessions today, thanks to the slyness of Hormuzd Rassam.

Elsewhere in Mesopotamia, other diggers were busy, with less success. Loftus, the Englishman who had explored Warka in 1849, was digging lucklessly at Babylon, Warka and other sites in the south. Two Frenchmen, Fresnel and Oppert, were having no better fortune with those ancient ruins. At Qalah Shergat, Rassam's men and Place's were both contending for the right to dig, and several scuffles had resulted, but no antiquities were found. In 1854, Rassam temporarily retired from archaeology, and his place at Mosul was taken by Loftus.

The French had been successful at Khorsabad, though, and by the summer of 1855 had assembled 268 cases of sculptures to be shipped to Paris. These got down the Tigris safely to Baghdad, but at a place called Kurnah, between Baghdad and Basra, Arab bandits emerged and forced the boats and rafts to halt. When the bandits opened some of the cases and found that they contained nothing but "old stones" of no apparent value, they were so infuriated that they dumped all of the cases overboard! They sank from sight, and never were recovered, a staggering loss to the new science of Assyriology.

The Crimean War put a halt to all excavation in the Near East for the time being. It was almost twenty years before the next authorized excavation—though the natives of Mesopotamia, aware by this time that the antiquities of the ancient mounds did indeed have value to collectors, quietly continued to work. As Seton Lloyd observes in his history of Mesopotamian archaeology, *Foundations in the Dust*, "At Nimroud the sound of pick and shovel were still not infrequently heard. All pretense of historical research had now been abandoned, and the place of the archaeologists had been taken by commercial speculators. In this way during the eighteen-sixties at least two consignments of sculpture were dispatched to Europe by Baghdad merchants."

It was a time of consolidation, of examining the things that had already been found, and drawing conclusions. The revival of interest in excavation came in 1872, with George Smith's astonishing discovery of the Deluge tablets, and before long Europeans were once again digging up Assyria and Babylonia.

In this new wave of excavations, one of the busiest men was Hormuzd Rassam, growing old but still active. As "Supervisor of Excavations" for the British Museum, Rassam was involved in a host of projects. He dug at Nimroud from 1878 to 1880, at Kouyunjik during the same years, at Qalah Shergat, at Babylon, and at various other sites in southern Mesopotamia. His old comrade Layard was Ambassador to Turkey during much of this time, and Rassam got Layard to use his influence in his favor, gaining official permission from the Sultan to explore the ancient mounds. Layard had arrived in Turkey at a time when the current Sultan was extremely reluctant to allow excavation at all. But on Rassam's behalf, Layard wangled a *firman* granting Rassam the right to excavate almost anywhere in the Turkish Empire, and to keep all he found (for shipment to England) except duplicates, which would go to the museum at Constantinople.

It was a vast territory, and Rassam tried to cover it all. The result was that he could not be everywhere at once, had to rely on sometimes incompetent local supervisors, and a good deal of damage was done during the excavations. Some important finds were made during Rassam's four years of work under this new *firman*, however. But he was thwarted in an attempt to dig at the sacred mound of Nebbi Yunus. He had actually begun to dig there before the religious authorities of Mosul forced him to halt.

To this date, nobody has managed to excavate Esarhaddon's palace at Nebbi Yunus. There it remains, beneath the doubtful shrine of the prophet. Elsewhere in Mesopotamia, though, a tremendous amount of work has been carried out, using techniques that would astound old Layard if he could see them.

One such site was Niffar, where Layard had worked briefly in 1850. He had been pessimistic about the value of the mound there. But from 1889 to 1900 an expedition sponsored by the University of Pennsylvania excavated at Niffar, which they discovered to be the site of the ancient Sumerian city of Nippur. Once again Layard had jumped too quickly to a conclusion about a southern Mesopotamian site. Nippur was a sacred city in old Sumer, and the American expedition came upon a priceless find: the temple archives, covering a period of more than a thousand years beginning about 2500 B.C.

Some 30,000 cuneiform tablets were found at Nippur, all of them a thousand years and more older than the tablets of Nineveh. Of this great horde, 2100 tablets were devoted to Sumerian literature, and in recent years the publication of Sumerian hymns and myths from Nippur has added greatly to our appreciation of Sumerian culture. So vast was the Nippur horde that today, decades after its discovery, it still has not been completely translated.

It is just as well for us that Layard failed to find the library of Nippur. With archaeology still in its primitive era, he might have done great damage to the irreplaceable archives. Most of the tablets were of unbaked clay, which had become soft as cheese over the millennia. They needed special handling if they were to be preserved.

One of the catastrophes of archaeology took place in 1881, when Hormuzd Rassam came upon a tablet-horde at the Sumerian city of Sippar. Many of these tablets simply crumbled away when Rassam attempted to remove them. Others were sent to the British Museum, where a so-called "expert" attempted to bake them for permanent preservation. He was unaware that salt had filtered into the clay over the years, and as soon as he put the tablets in the oven, a chemical reaction took place that turned the surface of each tablet to dust, and the inscriptions were lost forever.

By the time the Americans found the Nippur tablets, late in the nineteenth century, techniques for preservation had, luckily, been developed. Later archaeologists have learned to take great care with their finds. Consider Leonard Woolley's account of the treatment of tablets in his excavations at Ur in the 1920's:

"At Ur any lumps of clay looking like tablets are lifted from the ground still encased in their covering of earth, and are packed in metal boxes filled with clean sand; after they have been left for a few days to give the clay a chance to dry, the boxes are put into a rough-and-ready kiln heated by vaporized crude oil and are baked until the tins are red-hot and the clay is turned into terracotta. Then the tablets are taken out . . . the faces can be cleaned by brushing without any risk to the legibility of the characters."

Layard, being a pioneer, could not have imagined that any of this was necessary. It would have been tragic indeed if he had come across the fabulous archives of Nippur in 1851, only to bring about their unintentional destruction.

Aside from negotiating on Rassam's behalf, and playing an important role in obtaining a *firman* permitting the great German archaeologist Heinrich Schliemann to make his famous excavation of Troy, Layard took no interest in the work he had originated in the Near East. The archaeological chapter of his life was ended. In 1891, a young archaeologist wrote to Layard for some information about Assyria, and was told by the old traveler that he was "out of touch" with recent developments, and could be of no assistance. But the following year, Layard, then 75, wrote to the *Times* of London to express his displeasure at the way the Assyrian sculptures at the British Museum had recently been rearranged. (He was told that the rearrangement had been necessary, "to provide space for a lecture-room.")

Turkey was on the losing side in World War I, and after that war the Turkish Empire was dismembered, and a host of new countries emerged. The ruined cities of Assyria and Babylonia now became the property of the Kingdom of Iraq. The Turks had taken little interest in archaeology, except to place malicious obstacles in the paths of the various Europeans who wanted to dig in Mesopotamia. The new Iraqi government rightly came to see that the ruins of the dead cities were part of Iraq's national heritage, and began to take an active part in the program of excavation. Foreign expeditions were still permitted to work in Iraq, but they had to agree to share their finds with the Iraqi Department of Antiquities. By 1936, the first native Iraqi archaeologists were at work in the field, and today both foreign and Iraqi expeditions are busily continuing the enterprise that Botta and Layard began a century and a quarter ago.

The sites where those pioneers dug have been revisited,

with exceptional results. Luckily for today's archaeologists, Layard and his contemporaries never had time to make complete excavations at any of their mounds. Modern techniques of archaeology have found much that the first excavators overlooked. At Khorsabad, the University of Chicago worked from 1929 to 1935. Nimroud has been the site of work by the British School of Archaeology in Iraq since 1949, under M.E.L. Mallowan. Mallowan found, among other things, some superbly engraved ivory pieces which, thanks to modern preservative chemicals, did not fall to pieces "immediately on exposure to the air," as Layard had written so often and so dolefully. Kouyunjik was explored again by the British Museum under L. W. King and R. Campbell Thompson from 1903 to 1905, then by Thompson again from 1927 to 1932. More recently, British Museum workers have returned to the mound, have discovered another Assyrian palace, and have reached some of the earliest levels of Nineveh, more than four thousand years old, long before Assyria's time of glory. Qalah Shergat was excavated by Germans under Robert Koldewey and Walter Andrae between 1903 and 1914.

Today archaeology is an exact science, which calls for the strictest discipline. There have been many wonderful discoveries in the twentieth century, and the veil has been rolled back from much of what was once thought to be the forgotten past.

Yet with the coming of the scientific approach, some of the wonder and excitement of archaeology has departed. The field reports of modern archaeologists do not make thrilling reading, except to other archaeologists. The days of glamor, the days of bold ventures into the unknown past —those were Layard's days, more than a century ago, and those days will not come again.

We can go back, though, and see the mounds of Assyria through Layard's eyes, and share with him the spine-tingling pleasures of unearthing the palaces of Sennacherib and Assurnasirpal and Esarhaddon. Let us take a last look at him as he strolls over the mound of Nimroud on a spring day in 1847. He leaves his tent on the plain and ascends the mound. No ruins are visible yet, not a stone protruding from the soil. A broad level platform confronts him, and low black heaps, the tents of the Arabs.

Then a trench appears. A rude flight of steps leads into the bowels of the mound. Layard descends twenty feet, and finds himself between a pair of colossal lions, winged and human-headed. They form a gateway to an underground labyrinth.

Within, all is confusion. Arabs run madly about, some carrying baskets of earth from the pit, others carrying water-jugs to the diggers. Husky Nestorians wield the picks, raising clouds of fine dust at every stroke. Layard passes through the outer chamber, into a vast hall. On both sides of him are sculptured gigantic winged figures, some with the heads of eagles, others human in form. For an hour or more, he wanders through the halls of the palace, his eyes dazzled by long rows of sculptured kings, by figures of captives bearing objects of tribute, by enormous bulls and lions. In every chamber are new scenes of wonder and surprise.

At length, tired, Layard climbs up a row of stairs on the opposite side from where he entered, and finds himself once again on the platform, outside the excavation. We can turn to his own words now:

"We look around in vain for any traces of the wonderful remains we have just seen, and are half inclined to believe that we have dreamed a dream, or have been listening to some tale of Eastern romance.

198

"Some, who may hereafter tread on the spot when the grass again grows over the ruins of the Assyrian palaces, may indeed suspect that I have been relating a vision."

BIBLIOGRAPHY

Very little of the dialogue in this book is my own invention. Most of it is either taken directly from, or else somewhat adapted from, conversations found in A.H. Layard's own books.

The chief source for this book has been the work of Layard himself. Layard's archaeological and traveling career is to be found in four of his books, two published in his youth, one in old age and one posthumously. These are:

Nineveh and Its Remains (London, 1849).

Nineveh and Babylon (London, 1853).

Early Adventures in Persia, Susiana, and Babylonia (London, 1887. One-volume abridgment, 1894).

Autobiography and Letters (London, 1903).

The reader who is interested in learning more about the general field of Assyriology can turn to these books by other authors:

Foundations in the Dust, by Seton Lloyd (Penguin Books, London, 1955). An excellent paperback survey of exploration in Mesopotamia from the beginning of the nineteenth century until the middle of the twentieth, with special attention to Layard and other pioneers.

The Antiquity of Iraq, by S.Aa. Pallis (Munksgaard, Copenhagen, 1956). This encyclopedic 800-page book tells all that anyone would ever want to know about the archaeology of Mesopotamia. For the serious adult reader only, however.

Explorations in Bible Lands, by H.V. Hilprecht (Philadelphia, 1903). Long out of print, but well worth searching for, because it is a fine account of nineteenth century archaeology in Mesopotamia and elsewhere, written by a leading archaeologist of the time.

The Rise and Progress of Assyriology, by Wallis Budge (London, 1925). Also hard to find, but a first-rate account of the subject by a foremost archaeologist.

Sumer, the Dawn of Art and *The Arts of Assyria,* both by André Parrot (Golden Press, New York, 1961). Two remarkably handsome volumes of Mesopotamian art and archaeology. Hundreds of fine plates, including many of the palace reliefs Layard found. Excellent bibliography, many maps, altogether a top-notch job.

The Greatness That Was Babylon, by H.W.F. Saggs (Hawthorn Press, New York, 1962). The most recent and one of the best of the many histories of the Mesopotamian kingdoms.

Abde Pasha, 173
Abd-ur-Rahman, Sheikh, 89, 110, 112-113, 116
Aberdeen, Lord, 62-64, 69, 121, 179-182
Abou Salman tribe, 80, 86-89, 110
Afghanistan, 11, 44
Ahmeel Pasha, 77
Ainsworth, 31, 33
Albania, 14, 61, 68-69
Aleppo, 11, 18-19, 25, 27
Alexander the Great, 116
Andrae, Walter, 197
Arabian Nights, The, vii-viii, 4, 10, 18, 30, 33, 36, 77
Armenia, 138
Asia Minor, 11, 16-17, 122, 140
Assur, 30, 106. *See also* Qalah Shergat
Assurbanipal, 146, 149, 154, 161, 191
Assurnasirpal, 145, 158, 198
Assyria, ix, 18, 27, 29-30, 33, 37, 42, 47, 56, 65-68, 77, 86, 88, 91, 94, 100, 106, 116, 118-120, 122-123, 125, 129-131, 133-141, 144-148, 152-154, 156, 158, 162-163, 171-172, 174-175, 184-186, 188, 190-191, 193, 196-199
Austen, Benjamin, 5-8, 54, 64
Austen, Nathaniel, 2
Awad, 74-76, 78-79, 86, 88-89

Baalbek, 27
Baasheikha, 86
Babel, 32, 141, 162, 164
Babylon, 28-29, 33, 37-38, 134, 141, 145, 161-165, 167, 193. *See also* Hillah
Babylonia, 28-29, 32, 37, 47, 75, 133-135, 137, 141, 163-164, 190, 193, 196

Baghdad, vii-viii, 10-11, 19, 27, 29, 32-33, 35-38, 40-41, 43, 50-56, 58, 85, 90, 93-94, 100-102, 106-107, 109, 115-116, 130, 134-135, 151, 161-162, 165, 167-169, 173, 179, 192-193
Bakhtiyari tribe, 44-47, 49, 54, 107
Basra, 51, 93-94, 115, 130, 151, 160-161, 192
Bavian, 170
Behistun Rock, 42-43, 133-135, 142
Beirut, 18, 55
Birch, Samuel, 126
Bisutun. *See* Behistun Rock
Bombay, 93, 130-131
Bosnia, 61
Botta, Paul Emile, 41, 56-58, 61, 65-70, 79, 81, 86, 88, 92, 94-95, 97-98, 108, 119, 122, 129-130, 132, 135, 141, 144, 190, 196
British East India Company, 32, 37, 54, 114, 134
British Museum, 33, 78, 88, 97, 99, 108, 117, 120, 125-126, 129, 131, 137-139, 151, 154-155, 161, 170, 176, 192-193, 195-197
British School of Archaeology, 197
Brockeden, William, 7
Bulgaria, 15
Byron, Lord, 31

Calah, 30, 34, 75, 144. *See also* Nimroud
Canning, Sir Stratford, 55-64, 68-70, 84, 91, 97, 105, 121-122, 129, 131, 138, 179-181, 187

Ceylon, 1-2, 8-10, 13, 40, 48-49, 54-55, 123, 130, 137
Chicago, University of, 197
China, 57
Constantinople, viii, 10-11, 15, 18, 55-56, 58-59, 61-64, 67-71, 85, 93, 105-106, 121-123, 131, 134, 137-138, 142, 172, 176, 179-181, 184, 187-188, 193
Cooper, 138, 142, 150, 159, 170
Coste, 41, 45
Cowley, Lord, 121
cuneiform script, 32, 34-35, 42, 57, 65-66, 68, 76, 79, 81, 90, 100, 129, 132-137, 139, 152-153, 166, 190
Cyrus, 116

Damascus, 11, 25-26, 55, 188
Daoud Agha, 81-84
Darius, 134
Dead Sea, 19, 21, 24
Deluge of Noah, 155-158, 193
Derby, Lord, 178-179, 185-186
Destruction of Sennacherib, The (Byron), 31
Diarbekir, 173
Diodorus Siculus, 126-127
Discoveries in the Ruins of Nineveh and Babylon (Layard), 176-177
Disraeli, Benjamin, 6-7, 183, 186-187
Dur-Sharrukin, 66, 144. *See also* Khorsabad

Early Adventures (Layard), 137, 188
Elamites, 47, 134-135
Eridu, 165
Esarhaddon, 38, 145, 172, 187, 194, 198
Euphrates River, viii, 28, 158, 165

Flandin, 41, 45, 67, 98, 129

Florence, vii, 2-5, 122, 185
Foundations in the Dust (Lloyd), 192
Fresnel, 164, 192

Gebeil, 18
Geneva, 2
Gilgamesh, 156
Gladstone, William, 186
Gomel River, 170
Granville, Lord, 178
Grotefend, Georg Friedrich, 132-134
Guest, Enid, 187, 189

Hafiz Pasha, 85, 90
Hamadan, 43-44
Hammun Ali, 34
Hammurabi, 29, 37
Hezekiah, 147-148
Hillah, 32, 37, 162, 165. *See also* Babylon
Hincks, 135-137, 144-145, 153

India, 11, 44, 50, 93, 117, 130-131, 133, 184
Inscriptions in the Cuneiform Character from Assyrian Monuments (Layard), 129
Iraq, 196-197
Isfahan, 11, 44-45
Ismail Pasha, 85-87, 89-90

Jehu, 100
Jerusalem, 19-20, 147
Jonah, 30, 32, 103, 126-128, 171
Judah, 147-148
Judea, 19

Kalhu. *See* Calah
Karamles, 86, 127-128, 144
Karun River, 55
Kerak, 21-24
Kermanshah, 41-42, 133
Khabar River, 151

Khorsabad, 41, 65-67, 69, 76, 81, 86, 88, 93, 95, 101, 108, 120, 127-129, 141, 144, 190-192, 197. *See also* Dur-Sharrukin

Kiamil Pasha, 140

King, L. W., 197

Koldewey, Dr. Robert, 164, 197

Konia, 16

Kouyunjik, 32, 34, 57, 65, 68-69, 92, 101, 103, 105, 118-119, 125-128, 131, 138-140, 142, 144-148, 151, 154-155, 159, 161, 170-172, 190-191, 193, 197. *See also* Nineveh

Kurdistan, 95-96, 125-126, 138, 160, 173, 176

Kurnah, 192

Lagash, 28, 165

Layard, Austen Henry:
  early years, 2-9
  explores Turkish Empire, 14-27
  first visit to Nineveh, 30-35
  travels through Persia, 40-50
  befriended by Sir Stratford Canning, 58-70
  digs at Nimroud, 71-117
  returns to England, 118-124
  second expedition to Kouyunjik, 138-160
  explores Babylon, Niffar and Nebbi Yunus, 161-174
  political career, 175-199

Layard, Charles, 1, 8, 10

Layard, Daniel Peter, 1

Layard, Dean, 1

Layard, Enid. *See* Guest, Enid

Layard, Frederic, 2

Layard, Henry Peter, 1-3, 7-8

Lebanon, 11, 18

Lloyd, Seton, 192

Loftus, W. K., 167, 192

Longworth, 106

Louvre, 93, 108

MacNeill, Sir John, 12

Mallowan, M. E. L., 197

Malta, 122

Mehemet Taki Khan, 45-49, 54

Memoir on the Babylonian and Assyrian Inscriptions (Rawlinson), 136,

Mitford, Edward L., 10-19, 25, 27, 35-37, 40-44, 137, 161

Mohammed Keritli Oglu Pasha, 72-74, 79, 81-85, 140

Montenegro, 14

Monument de Ninive (Botta-Flandin), 129

Monuments of Nineveh (Layard), 129, 177

Mosul, viii, 27-35, 41, 56-57, 65-66, 68-69, 71-73, 77, 79, 82, 84-86, 89, 91-92, 94-96, 101-105, 108-109, 115-116, 118-121, 125, 127, 130, 133, 135, 137-140, 142-143, 151, 154-155, 159-161, 169, 171-175, 190, 192, 194

Nahr-el-Kelb, 27

Naples, 122

Napoleon, 2

Nebbi Yunus, 32, 35, 57, 103, 118, 127, 171-172, 194

Nebuchadnezzar, 38, 162-164

Niffar, 165-167, 194. *See also* Nippur

Nimroud, 33-35, 65, 68-69, 73-92, 94-95, 99-102, 106-108, 118, 120, 123, 125, 129-131, 140-146, 148-151, 158-159, 161, 170, 172, 190, 192-193, 197-198. *See also* Calah

Nineveh, vii, 18, 29-33, 65, 69-70, 75, 77, 122-123, 126-129, 133, 144, 146, 152, 154-156, 163, 174, 176, 178, 186, 188-189, 194, 197. *See also* Kouyunjik

Nineveh and Its Remains (Layard), 125, 127, 176
Nippur, 28, 165, 194-195. *See also* Niffar
Noah, 155-157

Oppert, Jules, 135, 192
Oxford University, 124

Palace of Sennacherib (Layard), 177
Palestine, 11
Palmerston, Lord, 121, 137, 183, 185
Paris, 2, 122
Pehlevi script, 133
Pennsylvania, University of, 194
Persepolis, 132-133
Persia, 11-12, 40-50, 54-56, 61-63, 116, 132-134, 142, 173
Petra, 21
Pisa, 2
Place, Victor, 190-192

Qalah Shergat, 34-35, 105-106, 151, 161, 169, 190, 192-193, 197. *See also* Assur

Rassam, Christian, 31, 33, 71, 108, 139
Rassam Hormuzd, 31, 86, 94, 116, 120, 138, 140, 142-143, 149-150, 154, 158-159, 161, 165, 167-169, 190-193, 195-196
Rawlinson, George, 127-128, 133, 144
Rawlinson, Henry, 90, 127, 133-137, 142, 144, 147, 155, 190-191
Rich, Claudius, 32-33, 37-38, 56-57, 162-163
Rome, 122
Ross, Dr., 52-53, 139, 175-176
Rouet, 80, 92, 119
Rucellai palace, vii, 4

Russell, Lord John, 178, 185
Russia, 63, 180-182

Sandwith, Dr., 138, 159
Sanna, 43
Sardanapalus. *See* Assurbanipal
Sargon I, 28, 30
Sargon II, 66, 144
Schliemann, Heinrich, 196
Schreiber, Lady Charlotte, 187
Scott, Sir Walter, vii, 4
Selamiyah, 75, 79-81, 83, 86
Sennacherib, 30-31, 37-38, 135, 142, 145-148, 152-156, 158, 160-161, 170-172, 191, 198
Serbia, 61
Shalmaneser I, 30, 144
Shalmaneser III, 100, 106, 151
Shereef-Khan, 172
Shishman, Toma, 119, 138-139, 152, 171
Sidon, 18
Sippar, 195
Smith, George, 154-156, 158, 193
Spain, 186-187
Stratford de Redcliffe, Lord. *See* Canning, Sir Stratford
Sumerian culture, 28-29, 34, 75, 141, 153-154, 156-158, 165, 167, 194-195
Susa, 44, 47-48, 54
Syria, 11, 18

Tahyar Pasha, 90-91
Tak-i-Bustan, 41
Talbot, W. H. Fox, 135
Taylor, Colonel, 37, 54, 56, 134
Teheran, 43, 142
Thompson, R. Campbell, 197
Tiglath-Pileser, 30
Tigris River, viii, 27-28, 32-35, 38, 73, 77, 85, 91, 93, 103, 105, 115, 119, 132, 158, 161-162, 192
Tripoli, 18

Troy, 196
Turkey, viii, 11, 14-18, 43, 55,
  57, 61-63, 68, 71-73, 140, 172,
  180-182, 187-188, 193, 196
Tyre, 18-19,

Ur, 28, 158, 165, 195
Uruk, 165, 167
Utnapishtim, 156

Vernet, Horace, 18-19
Victoria, Queen, 186, 188

Warka, 166-167, 192
Waterloo, Battle of, 2
White, Colonel, 64
Woolley, Sir Leonard, 97, 158,
  195

Yezidis, 96, 126

Zab River, 149
Zibbliyah, 167-168
Ziggurat, 141, 146

ABOUT THE AUTHOR

Robert Silverberg is a free-lance writer particularly well-known for his science-fiction books for adults, as well as for young people. Mr. Silverberg has published stories in all the top science-fiction magazines and is the author of *Time of the Great Freeze* and *Lost Race of Mars*.

Mr. Silverberg's interest has recently turned to the writing of nonfiction for young people, in both archeological and historical fields. THE MAN WHO FOUND NINEVEH is one of several of his books exploring the discoveries of vanished civilizations. He had traveled extensively to visit archeological sites both in the United States and overseas.

A graduate of Columbia, Mr. Silverberg, his wife (an electronics engineer who has done government work in radar and optics), and a number of pet cats share a large old Riverdale house that was once the home of Mayor Fiorello La Guardia.